The Wines and Vines of Europe

The Wines and Vines of Europe

by Howard L. Blum

A Benjamin Company/Rutledge Book

A Benjamin Company / Rutledge Book
Library of Congress Catalog Card Number: 72-97409
ISBN: 0-87502-027-5
All rights reserved
Produced by The Ridge Press Inc.–Rutledge Books Division
Published by The Benjamin Company, Inc.
485 Madison Avenue
New York, New York 10022
Printed in the United States of America

Copyright © 1974 by Howard L. Blum

Table of Contents

An Introduction to Imported Wines

THE HISTORY OF WINE

The knowledge of wine-making is so ancient that it is almost impossible to trace it back to its origins. We do know that wine was being produced in Egypt around 2400 B.C. and also in China at about the same time. In addition, there are many references to wine in the Old Testament. As civilization spread from the Far and Near East to the shores of the Mediterranean, wine-growing also spread and reached its first great heights in Greece along with its glorious civilization. From Greece the knowledge of wines spread to Rome, where Dionysus, the Greek god of wine, became the Roman god Bacchus.

It was the Romans who spread their knowledge of viticulture and vinification throughout all western Europe during the era of the Roman Empire. However, while the Romans were the first to spread wine-growing throughout that area, the Church's influence was the most important in the development of wine-making and in improving the quality of wine. The Church's interest stemmed from its requirement for sacramental wine, and since it was concerned with high quality, the wine-making methods of the Church continually raised the standards of all wine-making.

Much evidence of the magnitude of the Church's

influence still remains—such as the great Steinberg vineyard in the German Rheingau, which was first planted by the Cistercian monks over 700 years ago, and the famous Clos de Vougeot vineyard in France's Côte d'Or, which was also first planted by the Cistercian monks in the 12th century. Possibly the best example of the Church's influence is the vineyards at Châteauneuf-du-Pape, which were originally planted by Pope Clement V when he established the Holy See at Avignon.

The influence and power of the Church grew steadily greater throughout the Middle Ages and the Renaissance until at one time the Church owned most of the great vineyards of Europe. This domination continued in France until the French Revolutionary Assembly forced the secularization of the Church's property in its Act of July 12, 1790. This stripped the Church of all its great lands and power and caused many of the great vineyards to be divided up among a number of individual owners. This was particularly true in Burgundy, which accounts for so many small individually owned vineyard parcels in the Côte d'Or.

American viticulture also had an important influence on the vineyards of Europe. The first vines had been planted in California by Spanish missionaries who brought vine cuttings with them from Spain. Later, between 1858 and 1863, many American vines were reexported to Europe for experimental purposes, but, most disastrously, these vines brought with them the devastating phylloxera, native American plant lice that lived on the American root stocks. The phylloxera soon became the scourge of the European vineyards and destroyed most of them, from France down to Greece and from Spain over to Germany.

Every known pesticide was used to fight the disease but none was effective. Finally, Victor Pulliat, the great French writer on wines who lived in Chiroubles, theorized that if American root stocks were immune to the phylloxera, then the solution was to graft American root stocks onto European vines and thus defeat the phylloxera plague. When the first such grafts were made in Chiroubles, they proved the theory valid and thus provided the one effective method of defeating the phylloxera.

The vintner's life is both difficult and arduous, as well as uncertain, because traditionally vines have usually been planted in those areas where other crops wouldn't grow—either in very poor soil or on rocky hillsides. This unhappy circumstance will always exist, because it seems to be a quirk of nature that the harder the vine has to struggle, the finer the grapes it produces. The vintner must also constantly battle the elements—hoping for the right amount of sunshine and rain to produce a perfect crop and then waiting for the ideal time to start the vintage. At times, this is like playing Russian roulette—leaving the grapes on the vine for that vital and final maturing that produces the great wines, while always running the risk of an early frost that might well destroy the entire crop. But when everything is right, the result is a great vintage year and a great wine.

THE MAKING OF WINE

*I*n scientific terms, grape juice becomes wine as a result of the natural process of fermentation, during which the grape sugar is transformed into alcohol and carbon dioxide. The process occurs only in the presence of a yeast, which acts as a catalyst, inducing the reaction without taking part in it. The specific yeast in the fermentation of grape juice is known as saccharomycetes. This fungus settles on the outside of the skins of the grapes when they first begin to ripen, but starts its action only when the grape skins have been broken, either by crushing or pressing.

The precise time to start the vintage is the most delicate of all decisions the *vigneron* must make. The last two weeks of maturing can make a tremendous difference in both quality and quantity. Vintaging too early, to avoid a frost, can ensure a good yield, but it may be too low in alcohol for the desired quality. Waiting the precious extra week or two will give the grapes the necessary time to develop additional sugar, but a quick frost could spell disaster. In the Middle Ages, this delicate decision was made by the lord of the manor. He set the *ban de vendange*—the date before which the vintaging could not begin, with fines levied on those farmers who did not obey.

Once the date has been set, all available men and women from eight to eighty take part in the vintage to complete it as rapidly as possible, often working through the night to avoid any damage from frost. This is the culmination of all their labors over the spring and summer, and the fruits of their labors must be realized.

The vintagers collect the grapes in large baskets carried on their backs. Standing by in the vineyard is a horse-drawn, two-wheeled cart with a large wooden barrel into which the vintagers empty their baskets. The grapes are then taken to the press house where a mechanical crusher breaks the skins so that both juice and skins flow freely into the fermenting vat. In the case of red wine, the color comes from the skins of the grapes, which must be left in contact with the ferment-ing juice; the alcohol extracts the color from the skins.

Fermentation begins immediately and violently as a natural process, catalyzed by the saccharomycetes that were on the grape skins. The sugar in the grape juice is fermented into alcohol and carbon dioxide, which gives the juice the appearance of boiling. "To ferment" derives from the Latin *fervere,* which means "to boil." As soon as the first violent fermentation has subsided, the new wine is pressed, then "racked" and drawn off into clean barrels (called *barriques* in Bordeaux), where secondary fermentation continues until all the sugar has been converted into alcohol.

During fermentation in the barrel, a special type of water valve is used which permits the carbon dioxide to bubble out without any air entering. When fermentation is complete, the water seal is removed and the bung is driven home to permanently seal out any air. While the new wine is first maturing, it throws off impurities, known as "lees," that settle at the bottom of the barrel. The new wine must be racked clean into fresh casks to remove it from the lees, a process usually done three times in the first year.

The third racking is normally done in October, when the wine is one year old. The casks are then filled to the top and the bung driven home, and the wine is allowed to rest before bottling in the spring. Prior to bottling, all tiny particles that may be held in suspension are removed by fining, a method of natural filtration using a coagulating agent, such as egg albumin, that creates a thin film that absorbs the material in suspension. As the film settles to the bottom, it leaves the wine brilliant and clear.

Because wine is a living thing, it can be as temperamental as a human being. Therefore, bottling must be done on a clear day to maintain the wine's clarity. And again, since it is a living thing, the change from the cask to the bottle is a shock to the wine, causing what is called "bottle sickness," which lasts perhaps three or four months until the wine becomes accustomed to the bottle. After this, the wine continues to develop in the bottle, and as it matures and improves, a sediment develops that indicates this aging.

THE CARE AND SERVING OF WINE

*S*ediment is a proper and desirable sign in a fine

wine, a necessary result of its maturing. Wine should be aged in the bottle by being placed on its side so that the cork stays moist and thus stops any air from getting into the bottle. Fine wines should preferably be laid down for aging in a cool place where the temperature is fairly constant. Then, perhaps a day before serving, stand the bottle up in your dining room so that the sediment will go to the bottom and the wine will slowly come to room temperature. About an hour before dinner, pull the cork and let the wine breathe before serving. After all, if it is an old bottle, the wine may have been cooped up for eight or ten years, so it needs to breathe.

A great wine, by definition, is one that has achieved the perfect balance of its three vital attributes—color, bouquet and taste—all three of which are important to its appreciation. First comes the color: You should hold the glass up to the light. The wine should be clear and brilliant, whether it is the deep ruby of a red wine or the gentle amber of a white wine. Then comes the bouquet: It will tell you a great deal about the wine before you taste it. You should swirl the wine gently around in your glass to help release its bouquet and then sniff into the glass to get the fullness of the bouquet. The sense of taste is greatly influenced by the sense of smell, which explains why appreciating the bouquet is so important. Then, finally, the taste: It helps to hold the wine in your mouth for a moment, before you swallow, to feel the body. Then swallow and savor the taste and the aftertaste.

Proper glassware is most important for the fullest appreciation of a fine wine. The proper wine glass should always have a stem and preferably an eight-ounce bowl. The glass should be filled only halfway, which permits you to swirl the wine around to release more bouquet. The stem on a wine glass is important because by holding the glass by the stem, rather than around the bowl, you can more fully appreciate the color, and, in chilled wines, the warmth of your hand will not warm the wine.

THE WINE REGIONS OF ITALY

*T*he vineyards in Italy are the oldest in Europe, since the early Romans were great growers of the vine, cultivating it first in Italy and then throughout the entire Roman Empire. Today the vineyards in Italy extend almost continuously from the foot of the Alps in the north down to the subtropical southern tip of the boot. Italy is virtually one vast vineyard, and almost 25 percent of the entire population is active in one way or another in the wine industry, which explains why Italy today is the largest wine-producing country in the world, running slightly ahead of France. There is such a profusion of wine of all types and qualities from Italy that only the important regions, together with their best-known wines, can be mentioned:

1. PIEDMONT—Barolo, Barbaresco and Asti Spumante
2. LOMBARDY—Sassella and Frecciarossa
3. VERONA—Bardolino, Valpolicella and Soave
4. EMILIA-ROMAGNA—Lambrusco
5. TUSCANY—Chianti, Bianco Toscano and Vino dell'Elba
6. MARCHE—Verdicchio
7. UMBRIA—Orvieto
8. LATIUM—Est!Est!!Est!!! and Frascati
9. CAMPANIA—Lacrima Christi and Falerno
10. SICILY—Marsala and Corvo

THE WINE REGIONS OF FRANCE

*F*rance is now the second-largest wine-producing

country, but it is still the greatest producer of fine-quality wines in the world. The viticulture regulations of France are by far the most methodical, and they completely define, classify and control all of its many wine-producing regions.

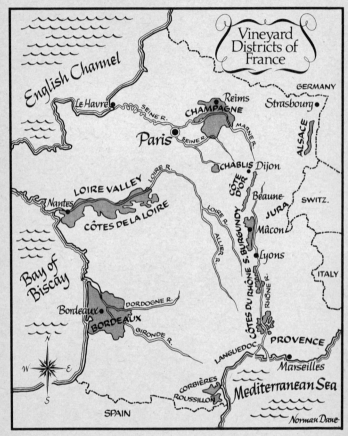

1. BORDEAUX (Gironde)
   a. *Médoc*—Renowned for majestic Clarets, this district is divided into fifty-three parishes, of which the most important are St. Estèphe, Pauillac, St. Julien and Margaux.
   b. *Graves*—Best known for white Graves and also fine Clarets.
   c. *Sauternes*—Comprised of five parishes, includ-

ing Barsac, all of which produce the rich, luscious Sauternes.

d. *St. Emilion and Pomerol*—Produce full-bodied red wines that are known as the "burgundies" of Bordeaux.

e. *Côtes de Blaye, Côtes de Bourg, Entre-deux-Mers and Premières Côtes de Bordeaux*—Large-producing areas on the eastern side of the Gironde and Garonne rivers, whose wines, both red and white, are somewhat less distinguished.

2. BURGUNDY (Côte d'Or)

a. *Côte de Beaune*—The principal parishes are Chassagne-Montrachet, Puligny-Montrachet, Meursault, Volnay, Pommard, Beaune, Pernand-Vergelesses and Aloxe-Corton.

b. *Côte de Nuits*—The principal parishes are Nuits-St. Georges, Vosne-Romanée, Flagey-Echézeaux, Vougeot, Chambolle-Musigny, Morey-St. Denis and Gevrey-Chambertin.

3. CHABLIS (Yonne)

a. The four appellations are *Grand Cru, Premier Cru,* Chablis and Petit Chablis.

4. SOUTHERN BURGUNDY (Saône-et-Loire)

a. *Côte Chalonnaise*—The important communes are Rully, Givry, Mercurey and Montagny.

b. *Côte Mâconnaise*—The most important appellation is Pouilly-Fuissé.

c. *Beaujolais*—The nine important communes are St.-Amour, Juliénas, Moulin-à-Vent, Chénas, Fleurie, Chiroubles, Morgon, Côte de Brouilly and Brouilly.

5. CHAMPAGNE (Marne)

a. Predominately black Pinot Noir grapes are grown north of the Marne River around Ay, Hautvillers and in the Montagne de Reims.

b. Predominately white Pinot Chardonnay grapes are grown south of the Marne around Cramant, Avize, Le Mesnil and Vertus.

6. ALSACE
   a. The important wines of Alsace are Riesling and Gewürztraminer.
7. LOIRE VALLEY
   a. The most important wines of the Loire Valley are Pouilly-Fumé, Sancerre, Vouvray, Anjou, Saumur and Muscadet.
8. RHONE VALLEY
   a. The five important areas are Côte Rôtie, Condrieu, Hermitage, Châteauneuf-du-Pape and the twin communes of Tavel and Lirac.
9. PROVENCE
   a. The five appellations are Palette, Bellet, Bandol, Cassis and Côtes de Provence.
10. SOUTHERN FRANCE
   a. The important V.D.Q.S. wines are Languedoc, Corbières and Roussillon.

THE WINE REGIONS OF GERMANY

The great vineyards on the Rhine and Moselle are the most northerly vineyards in all Europe. As if to make the vintners' tasks more arduous, most of the finer vineyards are on the steep terraced banks of these two rivers, on such difficult terrain that were it not for the vineyards, there would probably be nothing but forest and bare mountains. The three main wine-producing regions are classified and subdivided as follows:

1. RHINE VALLEY
   a. *The Rheinpfalz*—Also called the Palatinate—a triangular-shaped area between the Rhine, the Haardt Mountains and the French border.
   b. *The Rheinhessen*—Includes the left bank of the Rhine from Worms to Bingen.
   c. *The Nahe*—Includes the valley on both sides of the Nahe River up to the Rhine.

d. *The Rheingau*—Includes the right bank of the Rhine from Hochheim on the Main River to Lorch on the Rhine.
2. MOSELLE VALLEY
    a. *The Upper Moselle*—From the Luxembourg border to Leiwen, including the vineyards on the Saar and the Ruwer Rivers.
    b. *The Middle Moselle*—From Leiwen to Enkirch.
    c. *The Lower Moselle*—From Enkirch to Coblenz.
3. LOWER FRANCONIA
    a. Includes the area around Würzburg on the Main River.

THE WINE REGIONS OF SPAIN

*V*ineyards are planted throughout all of Spain, because although the soil is rather poor, the climate, which varies from almost tropical to temperate, is ideal for viticulture. Even though vines are cultivated in Spain on more land area than in any other country, Spain's wine production is only one-third that of Italy. This is the result of the Spanish custom of planting vines in a rather haphazard fashion mixed with other crops, instead of planting them in a precise, methodical manner. Except for the highly organized wine regions of Jerez and the Rioja, the wine regions in Spain are rather loosely defined. These are the most important regions:

1. JEREZ—The Sherry capital of the world.
2. MALAGA—Rather sweet and heavy wines, which are no longer very popular.
3. MONTILLA—Fortified wines somewhat on the style of Sherry.
4. LA MANCHA—Produces large quantities of lesser-quality, inexpensive wines.

5. TARRAGONA—Large production of nondescript red and white wines.
6. RIOJA—The finest-quality wine region, producing the "bordeaux" and "burgundies" of Spain and divided into three areas:
   a. *Rioja Alta*—Produces the lightest and finest Rioja wines.
   b. *Rioja Alavesa*—A smaller area whose wines are slightly stronger and less elegant.
   c. *Rioja Baja*—The largest producing area of the Rioja, whose wines are stronger, more coarse and generally of a lesser quality.

The Wines of Italy

In any discussion of the wine regions of Europe, it seems most logical to start with Italy, which was indeed the birthplace of modern viticulture and whose Roman legions spread the art of wine-growing throughout Gaul and western Germany. Back in the days of Pliny and Homer, Italy already led the then-civilized world in the quantity and excellence of her wines. The Romans had learned the art of making wine from the Greeks, had brought it back to Rome, and the vine soon became cultivated throughout Italy. The Romans not only borrowed the art of wine-making from the Greeks but they borrowed their god as well, changing Dionysus to Bacchus, who still reigns today as the god of wine.

Italy today is the world's largest producer of wines, with France running a close second. Italy is so well endowed by nature with a perfect climate and fertile soil that the vine grows abundantly everywhere.

The wine regions of Italy are not particularly well defined because before 1963 the government was not sufficiently active in defining the vineyard areas and regulating growths. For this reason, the nomenclature of Italian wines is often both varied and confusing, since wines were named after vineyard areas or towns or type of grapes or even vineyard owners. While this makes the study of Italian wines more difficult and at the same time more interesting, the best way to discuss the wines of Italy is to describe each department and the important wines it produces.

PIEDMONT

This is the most northerly department, lying in the foothills of the Alps, which protect the fertile valleys below from the winds and rain from the north.

In spite of the austere winters, the summers are warm and the autumns delightful, which accounts for Piedmont's producing some of Italy's finest wines, particularly red wines which come from the Nebbiolo grape.

Two of the best red wines are Barolo and Barbaresco, both of which are named for the villages in which they are grown. Both wines have somewhat the character of Châteauneuf-du-Pape—full bodied and robust, with a deep bouquet and a rich red color. Barolo is considered one of Italy's outstanding red wines. A somewhat similar wine is Barbera, which is produced on a much larger scale and named for its grape, to which the village name is often added. Barbera is a dark and tangy red wine, ideal with rich Italian food.

The vineyards around the town of Asti produce the well-known Asti Spumante, the delightful amber sparkling wine with a fruity taste and bouquet. Turin is important as well, not only as the capital of Piedmont but also as the capital of the Italian vermouth industry.

LOMBARDY

Lombardy is also a northern department of Italy, and it, too, is framed and protected by the Alps to the north. The finest wines come from the small Valtellina region, which is Italy's northernmost vineyard area, lying along the southern bank of the Adda River. These are delightful full-bodied red wines, also made from the Nebbiolo grape. Sassella has gained the greatest renown, but it is closely followed by Inferno and Grumello.

Farther south, near the town of Casteggio, is the famous hillside of Frecciarossa, where one Dr. Odero planted French vines many years ago and used French methods of viticulture. As a result, Frecciarossa is almost a château-bottled wine, in both the white and the red. The vineyards of Valtenesi, on the western bank of Lake Garda, are also important.

VERONA

The department of Verona, which extends westward from the town of Soave to the shores of Lake Garda, can best be described as "the garden spot of Italy." The ground is so fertile that it is almost one continuous vineyard from east to west. This is the home of Soave, one of Italy's most famous white wines. The vineyards grow on the hillsides surrounding the ruins of the medieval fortress that once protected the little town of Soave. Soave is a delightfully light yet fruity white wine, with a pleasant, subtle bouquet and an interestingly dry aftertaste.

North of Verona is Valpolicella, where again the vineyards are protected by low hills on three sides. Valpolicella is a fine ruby-colored wine with a delicate bouquet and a slightly bitter tang. It is just a bit heartier than its neighbor, Bardolino, where the vineyards lie along the eastern shores of Lake Garda.

EMILIA-ROMAGNA

The lush fertile plains of Emilia make it one of the largest wine-producing departments of Italy. Most of the red wines produced here come from the Lambrusca vine and hence are called Lambrusco, a bright-colored red wine with a pronounced bouquet, a slight touch of sweetness and a sparkle that quickly disappears. Most of the unfermented grape juice is shipped to the north, where it is used for making sparkling wines, because the floods of the Po River make it almost impossible to maintain dry cellars around Modena, the region from which Lambrusco comes.

TUSCANY

To most people, Tuscany is the home of Italian wines. The mere mention of Chianti is immediately associated with the familiar straw-covered flask. The name Chianti comes from a small area in the center of Tuscany, between the cities of Florence and Siena. Although mention of Chianti appears in old documents as early as 1260, officially the name dates back to 1378 when the Chianti League was instituted by an official act of the Republic of Florence.

Over the years, the name Chianti was used quite indiscriminately, not only for Chianti but also for almost any Italian red wine, mostly of a lesser quality. Finally, in 1924, in order to protect themselves, the wine-producers in Chianti formed the Chianti Consortium. They established rigid vinification controls and quality standards and required that all wine be submitted for examination. If the wine met the precise requirements established for Classico Chianti, then it was accorded the registered serialized trademark of the black cockerel, which was a guarantee of both quality and authenticity of origin. Thus, a Classico Chianti is often referred to as a "rooster" Chianti.

Reinforcing the Chianti Consortium, there was a ministerial decree in 1932, followed by a presidential decree in 1967, that further stipulated that the name Chianti belonged only to those wines produced from grapes grown in the clearly defined Chianti district.

Chianti is made from several grape varieties, principally the Sangiovese, but the vinification is slightly different. The first fermentation lasts five to ten days, after which the new wine is siphoned into smaller containers where the typical procedure of *Governo Chiantigiano* (Chianti process) takes place. This consists of putting into the container a small quantity of must from selected grapes, which was set aside earlier and dried. This starts a second and slower fermentation, at the end of which the wine acquires a fuller and more subtle taste.

Along with the indiscriminate use of the name Chianti, the traditional straw-covered flask also became associated with any Italian red wine and more often with those of lesser quality. However, the flask was a most unsatisfactory container because it was not only delicate and difficult to fill and pack, but also impossible to lay down for aging. Today, only less expensive Chianti is shipped in the traditional straw-covered flask ("fiasco").

Tuscany also produces several popular white wines —Bianco Toscano, which is a pleasant, clean and full-bodied dry wine; Vino dell'Elba, a very pleasant light white wine from the island of Elba; and Vin Santo, the traditional white wine of Tuscany, which is a rich, generous, sweet dessert wine with a delicate muscat flavor.

MARCHE

The Marche department lies quite exposed on the Adriatic Sea, and therefore not many great wines are grown in this area. One in particular is very important —Verdicchio dei Castelli di Jesi, which is produced on the hills of Ancona. Verdicchio is one of Italy's distinguished white wines, very pale and full of flavor and immediately recognizable from its vase-shaped bottle.

UMBRIA

The wines produced in Umbria are generally rather undistinguished, except Orvieto, which has earned a well-deserved reputation as one of Italy's most famous white wines. Orvieto is produced in the very small vineyard district of Orvieto in both *secco,* a delightfully dry wine, and the traditional *abboccato,* which is slightly fruitier, with a delightful bouquet. At one time, Orvieto was bottled in the traditional long-necked, straw-covered flask, but recently most of the important shippers have shifted to a squat oval bottle, reminiscent of the *Bocksbeutel,* which is far more convenient for chilling and serving.

LATIUM

This is the ancient province of Rome and the area in which the vine was first cultivated. Historically, the most famous vineyard area was called Dei Castelli and covered some fifty square miles on the volcanic hills south of Rome. From this area still comes Frascati, another popular Italian wine with a strong, fragrant bouquet and a dry finish. The tremendous cellars of Frascati date back to ancient Rome; a visit there is like a trip back 2,000 years.

27

Latium also produces a number of other quite unusual wines, of which the romantically named Est! Est!! Est!!! from Montefiascone on the shores of Lake Bolsena has an interesting history and a long-established reputation. In the 14th century, the German bishop Johann Fuger was on his way to the Vatican to pay homage to the pope. He sent his secretary-valet ahead to find suitable accommodations, with instructions to chalk the Latin word *Est* ("it is") on the wall of an inn where the food and particularly the wine were good. When the valet tasted the wines at Montefiascone, he found them so outstanding that he chalked on the wall "Est! Est!! Est!!!" The good bishop agreed so thoroughly that he returned from Rome and stayed permanently in Montefiascone.

The bishop's tomb is just within the entrance to the Basilica of St. Flaviano, carved with this inscription:

EST! EST!! EST!!! PROPTER NIMIUM EST
JOHANNES DE FUGER DOMINUS MEUS
MORTUUS EST

When translated, this roughly reads: "It is, it is, it is, and through too much of it, my master Johann Fuger is dead." Each year in August, the sentimental vintners of Montefiascone commemorate the anniversary of Bishop Fuger's death by spilling a barrel of Est! Est!! Est!!! over his tomb.

CAMPANIA

Historically, Italy's most famous wine is the storied Falerno, which was praised by many of the ancient Roman writers. Falerno still comes from Campania, but nowadays it is a rather undistinguished wine. Its availability today, however, symbolizes the strength of Roman viticulture, which has continued uninterruptedly for more than 2,000 years.

Presently the most famous wine of Campania is Lacrima Christi. Vineyards on the volcanic slopes of Mount Vesuvius produce this dry, golden-yellow wine with a velvety flavor and perfumed bouquet. Most of the Lacrima Christi is exported to the north, where it is made into sparkling wine. That produced in Campania remains a still wine.

SICILY

This is probably the oldest of all the wine departments of Italy. It was captured by Marcellus in 212 B.C. Syracuse was then the capital of Sicily, and Homer's *Odyssey* mentions how Ulysses escaped from the Cyclops who had fallen into a deep sleep from drinking wine.

Today, Sicily's most important wine is Marsala, from the western side of the island. The wine was first shipped to England in 1773 by John Woodhouse, who was a local exporter of various produce. Marsala is a rather sweet, fortified wine, deep brown in color, with a slight bitterness due to the volcanic type of soil. Its popularity dates back to the late 18th century, and for years England was its principal market.

29

The fertility and climate of Sicily are so ideal that some years ago the duke of Salaparuta planted an area on the western part of the island with Pinot Noir and used French methods of viticulture on his estate, which is called Corvo. The red wines of Corvo are some of the greatest of all Italy—fine, dry and rather austere, with some of the fiery nature of Sicily.

The Côte d'Or and Chablis

The history of the vine in Burgundy dates back to Caesar's conquest of Gaul, when the region we know today as Burgundy was part of the province of Gallia Narbonensis. The early records indicate that Beaune was made a fortified camp by the Romans around 40 B.C., and as the Romans conquered and settled there, they also planted the first vines, which they had brought with them from Italy. The people of Narbonensis were far more peaceful than in the other provinces of Aquitania, Lugdunensis and Belgica. They quickly became Romanized, and soon martial government was no longer necessary. In its place the province was ruled by a proconsul. It was during these peaceful "Romanized" years that the first vineyards flourished, laying the foundations for the great Burgundy wines we know today.

The name Burgundy was derived from the Germanic tribe of Burgundii, who were forced by the attacking Huns to flee their homeland on the Vistula. In 411, they sought refuge with the Romans in Gaul and quickly became their allies. As the Roman Empire was disintegrating, Burgundy was conquered in 613 by the Franks. There followed for 700 years a continuing battle over possession of the area, until it was finally returned to the Crown of France in 1363.

King John II gave the duchy of Burgundy to his son, Philip the Bold, and thus was started the auspicious era of the dukes of Burgundy who reigned supreme during the 14th and 15th centuries. Their great influence on Burgundy remains to this day, not only in the many Burgundian customs, but also in the large extent of the vineyards that although under separate appellations are still considered part of Burgundy.

While the Romans were the first to cultivate the vine in Burgundy, the important guiding and developing force came from the Church, which grew in power with the spread of Christianity. Noblemen and princes alike deeded great vineyards to the Church, which finally became so powerful that it rivaled the throne itself. This led to the revolutionary decree in 1790 that secularized the Church's property and forced it to break up and sell off its large holdings. This is the reason for the great fragmentation of vineyard ownership in Burgundy, where most vineyard owners have only small parcels of a given vineyard. Perhaps the best example of this is the famous Clos de Vougeot, which consists of 124 acres, of which there are seventy-two individual owners.

The powerful influence of the Church had a great effect on the development of viticulture. During the Dark Ages and the early Middle Ages, the Church was almost the only remaining seat of learning, and thus it alone carried on the art of viticulture during those barren years. The Church also spread viticulture when it founded new abbeys and planted vines in order to have wine for the sacrament. Since the fathers were far more interested in quality than in quantity, they continued to perfect the art and continually raised the standards that perforce were followed by the neighboring growers.

Although with secularization all the Church's lands were confiscated, some great vineyards remain today that date their origins back to the Church, such as Clos de Bèze, which was owned by the abbey of Bèze in the seventh century; Clos de Tart, which was started by the Bernardine nuns in 1260; and the famous Clos de

Vougeot, which was first planted by the Cistercian monks around 1150.

The important grape varieties used in Burgundy are very much linked with the very strict regulations of the *Appellation Contrôlée*. The basic law was enacted in 1905, strengthened in 1919 and finally completely defined in 1935. The most general designation is the "commune." All wines produced from vineyards in an individual commune are entitled to the "appellation" or name of that commune, such as Meursault, Beaune, Pommard, etc. Each commune is made up of small holdings called *climats* and where these have been designated as "first growths," the name of the *climat* may be used after the name of the commune, such as Beaune-Grèves, Pommard-Rugiens and Meursault-Charmes. And finally, the aristocrats are the *Grands Crus*, which may use their vineyard name all alone, such as Corton, Le Richebourg and Chambertin. A listing of the most important *Grands Crus* and *Premiers Crus* is included in the Appendix.

Since most of the vineyards in Burgundy consist of small parcels with individual owners, the Burgundians have adopted the system of "estate bottling." Technically, estate bottling guarantees only that the wine comes from one single *climat* owned by a single producer and that it has not been blended with wines from any other *climat*. Therefore, estate bottling is not automatically a guarantee of quality, but only a guarantee of origin and single ownership. The estate bottling designation becomes meaningful only when the estate itself has a reputation for producing a superior quality wine.

Since the entire system of *Appellation Contrôlée* in the Côte d'Or limits the areas that are entitled to use the specific commune designations, this also effectively limits the production of true Burgundy. Therefore, the Burgundian vintner is far more interested in quality than in quantity, and to this end grows the two noble grapes of the Côte d'Or: the Pinot Noir, which produces the majestic red wines, and the Pinot Chardonnay, from which the delicately dry, yet full-bodied white wines are made. Another much-used grape is the Gamay, which is planted only on the lower slopes and the upper parts of the vineyard, where, in most cases, only lesser Burgundies are produced. The wine made from a mixture of the Pinot and Gamay is known as *Passe-tous-grains.*

The heart of the true Burgundy region is the famous Côte d'Or, a narrow series of gentle hills running

northeast from Santenay in the south to Fixin in the north. The narrow vineyard area is never much more than half a mile wide and the entire length of the Côte d'Or is only thirty-six miles. The hills rise gently on both sides of the Route Nationale 74. The slopes on both sides of the road are almost completely covered with vines, so that in the fall, when the yellow leaves cover the vines, the gentle hills glisten in the autumn sun. Hence the designation Côte d'Or ("Golden Slope").

The southern part, called the Côte de Beaune, runs north from Santenay to Aloxe-Corton, and the northern part, called the Côte de Nuits, runs north from Pré-meaux to Fixin. As a general rule, the red wines of the Côte de Beaune are somewhat lighter-bodied, yet fruitier and mature somewhat sooner than those of the Côte de Nuits, which are heavier and bolder and take longer to mature. Also, most of the great white wines of Burgundy come from the southern communes of the Côte de Beaune, where the Pinot Chardonnay flourishes particularly well in the chalkier soil.

The most appropriate way to describe these two great areas is to detail each of the important communes together with their most famous *Grands Crus* and *Premiers Crus* vineyards. Starting from the southern tip, this is the arrangement of the important communes.

COTE DE BEAUNE

Santenay—The soil characteristics of Santenay are so varied that some of its red wines are full-bodied and deep-colored, similar to the Côte de Nuits, while others are somewhat lighter and more traditionally like the Côte de Beaune. The *climat* of Les Gravières is the only *Premier Cru* vineyard; its name comes from the stony soil rather typical of Santenay. While some San-

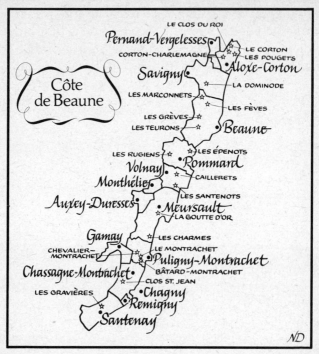

Côte de Beaune

LE CLOS DU ROI
Pernand-Vergelesses
CORTON-CHARLEMAGNE
LE CORTON
LES POUGETS
Savigny
Aloxe-Corton
LA DOMINODE
LES MARCONNETS
LES FÈVES
LES GRÈVES
LES TEURONS
Beaune
LES RUGIENS
LES ÉPENOTS
Volnay
Pommard
Monthélie
CAILLERETS
Auxey-Duresses
LES SANTENOTS
Meursault
LA GOUTTE D'OR
Gamay
LES CHARMES
CHEVALIER-
MONTRACHET
LE MONTRACHET
Puligny-Montrachet
BÂTARD-MONTRACHET
Chassagne-Montrachet
CLOS ST. JEAN
LES GRAVIÈRES
Chagny
Remigny
Santenay

ND

tenay red wines are sold under their commune name, most of them are sold under the appellation "Côte de Beaune-Villages."

VIN DE BOURGOGNE
CÔTE DE BEAUNE-VILLAGES
St Vincent
APPELLATION CÔTE DE BEAUNE-VILLAGES CONTRÔLÉE
Caves Chanson «Ancien bastion du XV° Siècle» à Beaune
CHANSON
PRODUCED, BOTTLED AND SHIPPED BY
CHANSON PÈRE & FILS, NÉGOCIANTS-ÉLEVEURS, BEAUNE (CÔTE-D'OR) FRANCE
1 PT. 8 FL. OZ.   PRODUCE OF FRANCE   ALCOHOL 11.5% BY VOL.

BURGUNDY TABLE WINE
TRADE   MARK
SANTENAY 1er CRU
« LES GRAVIÈRES »
APPELLATION SANTENAY CONTROLÉE
Prosper Maufoux
NÉGOCIANT A SANTENAY (COTE-D'OR)
Imported by :
THE HOUSE OF BURGUNDY
NEW YORK N. Y.
PRODUCT OF FRANCE   Net Contents : 12 Fl. Oz.

Chassagne-Montrachet—The rather stony and limy soil is very much in evidence in this commune as well as in the two neighboring ones of Puligny and Meursault. This is the special soil in which the noble Pinot Chardonnay flourishes so exceptionally and produces most of the great white Burgundies. The great *Grand Cru*, Le Montrachet, whose white wine has been famous since the 16th century, lies both in Chassagne and in Puligny, and hence both communes added this famous vineyard to their name around the end of the 19th century. Most of the white wines are shipped under the commune name of Chassagne-Montrachet and are known the world over for their dry, yet succulent flavor and flowery bouquet.

Puligny-Montrachet—This commune is the richest of all in possessing five *Grands Crus* white Burgundies. The most prestigious one is Le Montrachet, which is often called "the king of white Burgundies" because it possesses an almost unbelievable concentration of all the great qualities of that wine. This great *climat* is followed closely by Chevalier-Montrachet and Bâtard-Montrachet, and then the other *Grands Crus,* Les Bienvenues and Les Criots. Possessing such a wealth of *Grands Crus,* Puligny-Montrachet is justifiably famous for producing the finest white Burgundies.

Meursault—This is the last of the important white wine communes; its wines are slightly softer and less aristocratic than those of Puligny. Although Meursault contains no *Grands Crus,* two of its *Premiers Crus,*

37

Goutte d'Or and Charmes, are quite well known and highly respected. The white wines of Meursault have a high standard of quality, and they are sold primarily under their commune name.

Auxey-Duresses and Monthélie—These two neighboring small communes are often overlooked, even though they produce some very sound red wines that are typical of the Côte de Beaune. Their lack of popularity is probably because of their having previously been sold under the commune labels of Volnay and Pommard, a practice that was discontinued after the decree of *Appellation Contrôlée* in 1935.

Volnay—Here the soil changes again to favor the fine Pinot Noir, and with Volnay starts the progression of the great red wine communes, climaxing with Aloxe-Corton at the northern tip of the Côte de Beaune. Most of the finer red wines of Volnay are labeled Volnay-Santenots, as are the red wines from the vineyards on the northern side of Meursault; the white wines of Volnay are sold under the Meursault appellation.

Pommard—This is certainly the best-known name in Burgundy, probably because it is so easy to pronounce and hence has become Burgundy's most popular commune. There are no *Grands Crus* in Pommard, but the two *Premiers Crus,* Les Epenots and Les Rugiens, have certainly gained a worthy reputation. But by and large, the wines of Pommard are not as outstanding as their popularity would indicate, because that popularity usually results in their being overpriced.

Beaune—This is the largest commune in the Côte de Beaune and the city of Beaune—considered the capital of Burgundy—is also located here. In addition to a number of excellent *Premiers Crus,* such as Les Fèves, Les Grèves, Les Marconnets, Clos des Mouches and Les Teurons, Beaune is mainly famous for the singularly great Hospices de Beaune. This unusual institution was created in 1441, when Nicolas Rolin and his wife, Guigone de Salins, donated the property and the building funds. The Hôtel-Dieu was opened as a charitable hospital in 1443 and has been in continuous service ever since. It is a magnificent four-story, block-square building built in the Flemish style, with a high-pitched roof and dormers, all decorated with handsome multicolored Flemish tiles.

Nicolas Rolin and his wife also donated to the Hospices several parcels of fine vineyards so that their proceeds would enable the hospital to be self-supporting. In time, other rich benefactors followed Rolin's example and also donated other fine *climats,* so that the principal support for the Hospices de Beaune continues to come from the sale of wines from the parcels donated by wealthy Burgundians.

The annual auction of the Hospices de Beaune is held every year on the third Sunday in November in the magnificent open courtyard of the Hôtel-Dieu. The wines of the Hospices de Beaune comprise some twenty-nine different parcels, which are individually named *cuvées* after their donor. The prices paid for the different *cuvées,* while being somewhat higher because of the charitable aspect, nevertheless represent a sort of guide for the current vintage, since these wines are traditionally the first ones of the vintage to be sold.

Savigny-Les-Beaune—Because the little village of Savigny and its vineyards are somewhat off the beaten track, this commune is often passed by even though its red wines are very good indeed. Historically, Savigny was once quite important because it was the headquarters of many of the important wine shippers of the Côte de Beaune. The most important vineyard is the *Premier Cru,* La Dominode.

Pernand-Vergelesses—Unfortunately the very fine red wines of this commune suffer from being over-shadowed by the great wines of Aloxe-Corton. Its most famous vineyard is the *Premier Cru,* Ile des Vergelesses, and part of the famous Corton-Charlemagne also lies in this commune.

Aloxe-Corton—This commune presents the peak of the red wines of the Côte de Beaune, and many feel of the Côte de Nuits as well, since it boasts the home of the famous *Grand Cru,* Le Corton, which is the single great growth red wine of the Côte de Beaune. The other *Grand Cru* is Corton-Charlemagne, which is a magnificent white wine, most certainly equal to the finest of Burgundy. Another famous vineyard is the *Premier Cru,* Le Clos du Roi, which, by its name, indicates how regal this commune has always been. At first, this renowned vineyard belonged to the dukes of Burgundy, and later on to the king of France, from whom it derived its name.

Nuits-St. Georges and Prémeaux—These are the first two communes of the Côte de Nuits, of which the town of Nuits-St. Georges is considered the capital, where many shippers have their headquarters. None of the vineyards are particularly famous, and the wines of both communes are usually sold under the appellation "Nuits-St. Georges," or when blended with wines of some of the other Côte de Nuits communes, they are sold under the appellation "Côte de Nuits-Villages."

Vosne-Romanée—The little village of Vosne lies at the foot of the most famous vineyard area in Burgundy, the slowly rising long incline of reddish soil on which are the celebrated *Grands Crus* vineyards of Romanée-St.-Vivant, La Tâche, La Romanée-Conti, La Romanée and the highly regarded Le Richebourg. These are among the rarest and most prized *climats* in all of Burgundy.

Flagey-Echézeaux—While small in area, this commune is most important because of its two *Grands Crus,* Les Echézeaux and Les Grands Echézeaux. Because it is such a close neighbor to Vosne-Romanée, the other wines are permitted to use the more popular commune name of Vosne-Romanée.

Vougeot—This commune owes its great fame to the imposing *Grand Cru* vineyard of Clos de Vougeot, whose 124 acres make it the largest single *Grand Cru* in the Côte d'Or. Clos de Vougeot was first cultivated by the Cistercian monks in the early part of the 12th century, and the imposing Château de Clos de Vougeot was completed in the mid-16th century, serving both as a monastery and as the winery and cellars of this celebrated vineyard.

The decree of 1790 confiscated the lands and forced their sale to private individuals, so that today there are seventy-two different owners of parcels of this famed vineyard. After 1790, the great château passed through many hands and finally fell into disrepair. It was re-

43

stored in 1944 when it was taken over by Les Chevaliers du Tastevin. The Château de Clos de Vougeot now serves as the headquarters of this illustrious Order of Burgundian Wine Lovers and is the site of their impressive ceremonies.

There is an amusing story about Clos de Vougeot that dates back to Duke Philip the Bold. As he was surveying the vintage he noticed one of the women lagging well behind because she was apparently taking such great care in picking and selecting the grapes. The duke rode up on horseback and exclaimed to her that she must certainly be a great lover of Burgundy to be picking the grapes so adoringly and carefully. The young woman looked up and quietly replied, "No, sire, it is not I, but rather my husband who loves great Burgundy—but then, in the end, it is I who enjoy the best part."

Chambolle-Musigny—A large quantity of fine red wine is produced by this important commune, which is most famous for its two *Grands Crus,* Le Musigny and Les Bonnes Mares. Le Musigny is a very ancient vineyard dating back to the early 1100s and also ranks as one of the finest *Grands Crus.*

Morey-St.Denis—This commune got its name when the little village of Morey added the name of its most famous vineyard, St. Denis, which at one time belonged to the abbey of St. Denis. There are also two other *Grands Crus,* Clos de la Roche and Clos de Tart; the latter vineyard was given to the Bernardine nuns in the 13th century.

Gevrey-Chambertin—This is the largest commune of the Côte de Nuits and probably its most famous, because of its *Grand Cru* vineyard Chambertin, which has an ancient and interesting history. The first vineyard in this commune was planted by the monks of the abbey de Bèze, who were deeded the land in the seventh century. The wines of Clos de Bèze gained such fame that a neighboring farmer by the name of Bertin decided to emulate the monks and cultivate the same vines in his field. *Champ* is the French word for field—hence, *champ de Bertin,* and finally, Chambertin, as we know it today. Its prestigious *Grands Crus* are Chambertin, Clos de Bèze, Mazis-Chambertin and Charmes-Chambertin.

Brochon and Fixin—These are the last two communes of the Côte de Nuits. They do not produce any particularly distinguished wines, so most of their red wines are sold under the appellation "Côte de Nuits-Villages."

The region of Chablis is always considered part of Burgundy, even though it's about sixty-five miles northwest of the Côte de Nuits, in the separate department of Yonne. In the 12th century, when this region produced both red and white wines, the wines were known as the wines of Auxerre, the chief town of the department, and the name Auxerre was used until the 18th century. While red wines were then the principal production, the white wines of Chablis first gained their special reputation because of the vineyard created in 1142 at the abbey of Cîteaux at Pointigny, the vineyard that shaped the future of the wines of Chablis.

The real impetus given to wine production in Chablis came originally from its shipping accessibility to Paris via the Yonne River. This was such a great advantage that, by the 19th century, Chablis was the largest wine-producing region in all of Burgundy. When the phylloxera destroyed the vineyards, the Chablis region lost out to the better-yielding vineyards in the

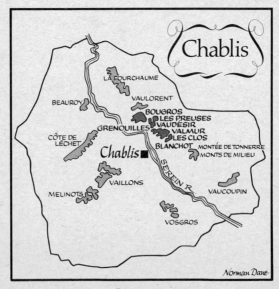

south, because the new railroads had made it economically possible to ship wines from the south to Paris. In self-defense, the wine-growers of the Yonne decided to restock only that portion of the Chablis area where the great white wines had been grown, thus starting their specialization in the individualistically crisply dry white wines of Chablis.

Chablis is a small town in the center of the region where the Serein River has cut a valley 450 feet below the low-lying hills on which the Chablis vines grow. There are seven *Grands Crus* vineyards in Chablis, which are all located on the northern bank of the Serein: Bougros, Les Preuses, Vaudésir, Grenouilles, Valmur, Les Clos and Blanchots. The *Premiers Crus* vineyards are scattered on both banks, but the most important ones, of which the best known is Mont de Milieu, lie just south of the *Grands Crus*.

The third appellation is Chablis, and the fourth is Petit Chablis. These four appellations of Chablis account for about 50 percent of the entire white wine production, with the balance made up of lesser wines, of which the best known is Bourgogne Aligoté.

Southern Burgundy

The region of southern Burgundy starts just to the east of Santenay and stretches southward along the west bank of the Saône River, down below Villefranche. The entire region is about seventy-five miles long and is divided into three separate areas: the Côte Chalonnaise, the Côte Mâconnaise and Beaujolais. The wines of these areas are quite different from one another because of the differing soil characteristics, and they are all becoming increasingly popular as the wines of the more prestigious Côte d'Or have become more expensive.

THE COTE CHALONNAISE

The northernmost region is the Côte Chalonnaise, which starts with the hills south of Santenay. The soil and terrain are similar to that of the southern tip of the Côte de Beaune, and consequently the wines have many of the same characteristics. It is unfortunate that the wines of this region have always been dwarfed by the more prestigious Côte de Beaune, because many of the wines of the Côte Chalonnaise are very creditable.

49

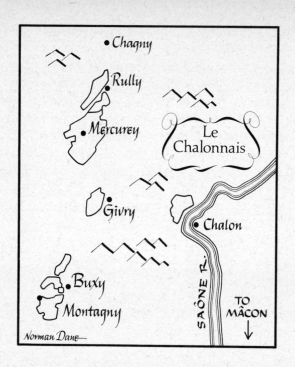

The Côte Chalonnaise is comprised of the four rather distinct communes of Rully, Mercurey, Givry and Montagny. The first is the ancient village of Rully, which is only fourteen miles south of Beaune and was apparently named after the Roman tribune Rullus, who was known for his far-reaching agrarian reforms. Rully produces primarily white wines that are rather perfumed and heady and therefore particularly adaptable to the making of sparkling Burgundy, which is an important wine trade of Rully.

Just a few miles south is the old Roman village of Mercurey, named after the Roman god Mercury. The red wines of Mercurey are indeed quite excellent and are considered by many to be almost the equal of those of the Côte de Beaune. Then, only a few miles farther south, is the town of Givry, the third commune, which also produces primarily red wines that are equal, if not slightly superior, to those of Mercurey. The last commune, which is farther removed to the south, is Montagny, which produces quite excellent white wines that closely rival the white wines of the Côte de Beaune.

THE COTE MACONNAISE

Going south and in the valley of the Saône River, the next region is the Côte Mâconnaise, which takes its name from its principal town of Mâcon, at the southern tip of the region. At one time, Mâcon was a tremendous red-wine-producing area, but today its great claim to fame is its southern pocket, so well known as Pouilly-Fuissé, where the rather limy soil is particularly well suited to the Pinot Chardonnay. The wines of Pouilly-Fuissé are pale and delicate, with a delightful fruity bouquet, very reminiscent of the white wines of the Côte de Beaune.

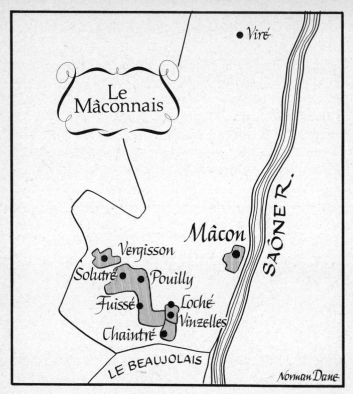

This particular region first got its name from the linking together of the neighboring villages of Pouilly and Fuissé. Today the appellation Pouilly-Fuissé includes the five neighboring communes of Pouilly, Fuissé, Vergisson, Solutré and Chaintré. Bordering on Pouilly-Fuissé are the two other important communes of Pouilly-Loché and Pouilly-Vinzelles, both of which produce similarly excellent wines, but they can be sold only under their own appellations and not as Pouilly-Fuissé.

In other designated areas of Mâcon, the white wines carry the designation of Mâcon Blanc, or the slightly higher designation of Mâcon-Villages, but both of these can also be labeled Bourgogne Blanc. The red wines of Mâcon are also important; they are generally lighter in body and bouquet than the wines of the Côte de Beaune. Of historical interest are the red wines of Tournus that were rated in the 14th century by Charles VI ahead of the Burgundies of Dijon.

BEAUJOLAIS

Just south of Pouilly-Fuissé starts the great Beaujolais, a rather large and very productive region that is forty-five miles long. It is really the "wine country of southern France" and is symbolically described by the saying that "three rivers wash Lyons—the Saône, the Rhone and the Beaujolais." Beaujolais got its name from the little town of Beaujeu, which was the seat of the province in the 12th century, until the new village of Villefranche was built nearer the Saône and became the capital of the province.

The special feature of the Beaujolais is that just south of Pouilly-Fuissé the soil suddenly becomes quite granitelike, which is particularly favorable to the Gamay grape that here produces the jubilantly light and cheery Beaujolais. The finest Beaujolais comes from nine communes that are all located in the northern part of the region, each of which is entitled to its own appellation. Rather than trying to classify these according to quality, it is better to describe each in order, starting in the north.

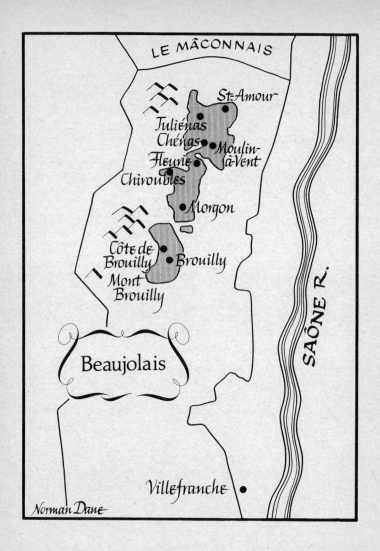

First comes St.-Amour, the northernmost commune, whose wines are very much prized because many
feel they combine the best qualities of the other eight
areas. In parts of St.-Amour, the soil contains some of
the limestone qualities similar to the bordering Pouilly
district, and this is responsible for the delightful Beaujolais Blanc, which is usually drier and more delicate
than Mâcon Blanc, but with slightly less body. The next

area is Juliénas, which is supposed to have been named after Julius Caesar; then to the south comes Chénas, named after the oak trees, *chênes*, that at one time covered all of Beaujolais.

Then comes the important locale of Moulin-à-Vent, whose wines are the best known and probably the finest in all of Beaujolais. Close by is Fleurie, probably so named because its wines are known for their flowery bouquet and delicacy. The next two areas are Chiroubles and Morgon. Chiroubles has a special significance as the home of Victor Pulliat, who was the first to suggest that American roots should be grafted to French vines to defeat the phylloxera plague.

The last two locales are Brouilly and Côte de Brouilly. Brouilly is the largest-producing of these nine areas, and its vineyards almost encircle Mont Brouilly. There the vineyards on its slopes make up Côte de Brouilly, whose wines are considered superior to those of Brouilly. Normally in Burgundy the designation "Côte de _____" denotes a lesser status, but here Côte de Brouilly outranks Brouilly.

Apart from these nine communes, whose production is rather limited, most of the wine produced in Beaujolais is labeled simply "Beaujolais." However, there are thirty-six specially designated communes that are entitled to the higher appellation "Beaujolais-Villages," denoting their superior quality.

One further observation—it appears to have become fashionable to sell Beaujolais almost before it's bottled, when it is really too young and too fresh to be appreciated. As light a red wine as Beaujolais may be, it still has quality, and as such it needs and deserves time, both in the barrel and in the bottle, to develop properly the freshness for which it is famed. While the people of Lyons drink Beaujolais virtually *en barrique,* this applies only to lesser Beaujolais, which are not big enough to warrant the time required to mature them. It's almost a sin to drink a good Beaujolais too young, before it has had time to develop.

The Wines of Bordeaux

The ancient Gallic province of Aquitania fell under Roman rule when Caesar's lieutenant Crassus conquered it in 56 B.C. and established Burdigalia as the chief city. With the coming of the Romans, the fame of Bordeaux became irrevocably linked with the excellence of its wines, for as they had done everywhere else in Gaul, the Romans brought with them the cultivation of the vine.

The Aquitani were a very independent and peace-loving people who diligently cultivated the vineyards as individual growers rather than as Roman slaves working on vast estates. This led to Aquitania's becoming a land of individual vineyard owners, each of whom lived on his own land in a so-called villa, a completely self-sufficient entity with its own winery, and its own cellars and pottery kilns.

After the end of the Roman era around A.D. 450, Bordeaux suffered, as did all of Gaul, from the ravages of warring would-be conquerors. Finally, in 1152, Eleanor of Aquitaine married Henry of Anjou, and two years later, when he became King Henry II of England, Bordeaux and all the vast duchy of Guyenne came under the domination of the English Crown.

During the 300 years of English rule, the wines of

Bordeaux entered their first great era of growth—in quality, fame and production. During this era, the term *Claret* first came into use, coined by the English to distinguish the clearer, lighter red wines of Bordeaux from the darker, heavier wines of the Rhone Valley that were then the popular wines in France. Because Bordeaux was under English rule, its wines enjoyed all the rights of the Crown, which in England gave them an important duty advantage over other French wines.

The tables were turned in 1453 when the English were defeated at the battle of Castillon, and Bordeaux and the entire province of Guyenne were recaptured by France. With this turn of events, Bordeaux not only lost its important English market, but was also left without a market in France to replace it. The city fathers decided to embark on what was perhaps the first systematic sales and public relations campaign in the history of wine. They visited all the courts of France and other influential centers, sending sample shipments in order to establish the quality and reputation of the great wines of Bordeaux. By the time of the French Revolution, this campaign had been so successful that Bordeaux wines had attained their rightful place in France.

The wine trade of Bordeaux had been developed by thousands of small independent vineyard owners. During the twenty-five years before the French Revolution, the city of Bordeaux ascended to great commercial heights, not only because of the worldwide reputation of its wines but also because it was France's most important Atlantic seaport. The crippling French Revolution brought an abrupt end to the important shipping industry of Bordeaux, but once again, the wines of Bordeaux came to the rescue of the city and its people. They went whole-heartedly back to their wines, expanding their vineyards and their sales throughout France, which eventually led to their preeminent position as the largest fine-wine district in the world, as well as the largest exporter of fine wines.

THE CHATEAU WINE TRADE

*W*ine-growing has always been the main occupation and the lifeblood of the people of Bordeaux, and the development of the château system stems from their custom of owning and working their own individual vineyards. The first such vineyards were planted in Graves, just outside the town of Bordeaux, and as other towns developed, again the new vineyards were clustered around them.

The concept of the château system had its first impact during the 300-year English rule from 1152 to 1453, when the English first made Claret popular. Since the Bordeaux wine trade had been developed by small individual vineyards, it followed that this system was further expanded during the trade with England. Whereas previously the vineyard buildings were nothing more than simple homes with a winery and cellar, it was during the "English" period that many of the great châteaux were first built—such as Margaux, Pape Clément, Yquem, Lafite, Mouton and Carbonnieux.

By the time the French finally drove out the English in 1453, the château system had become so firmly established that the French continued it and even elaborated on it. Then followed the flourishing of Bordeaux and, with it, the building of the more palatial châteaux that still grace many of the fine properties. After languishing during the bourgeois Jacobean period, Bordeaux and its wines flourished again, with many new châteaux, so that by 1855 there were over 4,000 individual châteaux in Bordeaux.

That date, 1855, is particularly significant because in that year, in order to present their wines at the International Exposition in Paris, the officials of the Bordeaux Chamber of Commerce asked the members of the Bordeaux Association of Wine Brokers to select the greatest châteaux. Since there was no unanimity of opinion, a jury was selected to classify the outstanding Clarets and Sauternes, based not only on their quality but also on their past reputations. A total of sixty-one Clarets (all from the Médoc except one from the Graves) were classified into five growths, and a total of twenty-five Sauternes were classified into two growths plus one superior growth. Although this classification was made over 100 years ago, by and large it still holds true today.

Since only the Clarets of the Médoc (except for Haut-Brion) were included in the 1855 classification, additional classifications were required for the other districts. The Clarets of the Graves, along with the white Graves, were finally classified in 1953, and the Clarets of St. Emilion were classified two years later, in 1955. For some reason, the Clarets of Pomerol have never been classified, but their own "unofficial classification" is commercially recognized by the Bordeaux Wine Trade. The complete classifications of Bordeaux châteaux are listed in the appendix.

While classifications are both official and reliable guides, it is important not to prejudge, nor be misled by, a wine having been classified as a first, second, third, fourth or fifth growth, or even in a lower classification. While it may be easy to differentiate between a classified Claret and a *Cru Bourgeois*, it is quite difficult to choose between a second and third growth or between a third and fourth growth. Furthermore, all too often people are prejudiced against one of the fifth growths, not realizing that these are still among the select few sixty-one châteaux that were classified in 1855. A wine may be very creditable without having an impressive classification, just as a classified growth is not necessarily always a great wine.

On the other side of the coin, just as it is important to recognize the reputation of one of the classified châteaux, one cannot unilaterally assume that any château designation is in itself a guarantee of quality.

Essentially the château designation is a guarantee only of origin, while the guarantee of quality depends upon the reputation of the château. With over 4,000 châteaux in Bordeaux, it stands to reason that many of these may be only mediocre wines that try to upgrade themselves by trading on their château designation. A château must develop its own reputation and stature on the basis of its quality and reliability.

The château system of vineyard ownership formed the backbone of the classification system and spread the fame of Bordeaux wines throughout the world. But in time, the multiplicity of new châteaux required more definition of the term, which was finally regulated by strict governmental decree in 1949. Basically, this decree established that the term *château* denoted a given viti-cultural holding and that the use of the name of the château was restricted to the wine produced by that property. By the very nature of the château system, each individual owner was basically and only a producer and not concerned with the marketing of his wines. This led to the formation of the Bordeaux Association of Wine Brokers, whose members form the marketing arm of the Bordeaux wine trade. These are the *négociants*, or shippers, who act as the sellers but not as producers.

Another term indigenous to Bordeaux is *en primeur*, which denotes the first sale. Traditionally, and particularly for the classified châteaux, in April of each year the new vintage is first offered *en barrique*, which indicates that the wine is still in the barrel. This will usually be the lowest price at which that particular vintage will ever be sold, because the terms require immediate payment even though shipment in the bottle will be made some eighteen months later.

Since most great châteaux start reaching maturity only after five or six years, and attain their peak only after ten years, purchasing *en primeur* requires holding the wine for at least three years after it has been shipped. The custom of laying down the great châteaux originated in England where cellars were handed down from father to son. In this way, a son would enjoy the fine wines laid down perhaps fifteen years previously by his father, and he would replace them by laying down new vintages for the next generation. This is the way to enjoy a fifty-dollar bottle that might have cost only five dollars fifteen years before.

PETITS CHATEAUX

*I*n recent years, along with increased demand and elevated prices, the designation *petit château* has become quite popular and more meaningful. While we have referred in detail only to the primary classifications of the Médoc, St. Emilion, Pomerol, Graves and Sauternes, these classifications comprise a total of only 162 châteaux. Since there are over 4,000 registered châteaux in Bordeaux, many of these were also classified, but in various lower categories for each district. As a group, these are now generally referred to as *petits châteaux*.

Before the recent upsurge in the popularity of Bordeaux, many lesser châteaux had been unable to develop their own market, so that they were usually sold under the shippers' labels, as superior quality regional wines. Recently, the increased demand for *petits châteaux* has enabled many of these lesser châteaux to be sold on their own merit, and many have developed creditable reputations for their sound quality, reasonably priced wine. However, one must realize that the château designation is not a guarantee of quality, but of origin. This is most important in the case of *petits châteaux,* where many lesser wines may be taking advantage of this unofficial designation in order to trade themselves up. As always, the value of the wine depends entirely on its quality and reputation, and not on its designation.

*B*esides making the market for château-bottled wines, the Bordeaux shippers do a considerable business in district wines, which do not have enough stature or quality to be sold as château wines. According to the regulations of the *Appellation Contrôlée,* the name of a parish or district may be used when all the wines come from only that parish or district. District wines need not come from only one vineyard but may be blended from several vineyards, provided again that they all come from the same parish or district. Understandably, a district wine will always be labeled with the highest designation to which it is entitled. For example, it may be labeled simply "Médoc" or, if it is so entitled, with a higher designation, such as "St. Estèphe" or "Margaux."

District wines are a very important trade for the Bordeaux shipper, who continually samples and buys young wines from the many small growers, blends them to his standards, ages them and finally bottles and ships them under his own label. Since these are all blended wines, the shipper's individual reputation is the only guide to quality in district wines. Because the leading shippers so zealously guard their long-established reputation for quality, the district wine from one of these leading shippers will quite often be superior to a more expensive, but relatively unknown, *petit château.* As such, the district wines from reputable shippers are often very good buys.

THE WINE DISTRICTS OF BORDEAUX

*T*he entire wine region of Bordeaux, in the department of Gironde, lies in part on the left bank of the Gironde River, on both banks of the Garonne River and on a part of the right bank of the Dordogne River. By wine-producing standards, it is an immense region, the largest in France, covering about one million acres and producing about seventy-five million gallons of wine annually, about equally divided between red and white. The five main quality-producing districts are Médoc, Graves, Sauternes, St. Emilion and Pomerol. In addition, there are a number of lesser-quality producing districts, of which the most important are Côtes de Blayes, Côtes de Bourg, Entre-deux-Mers and Premières Côtes de Bordeaux.

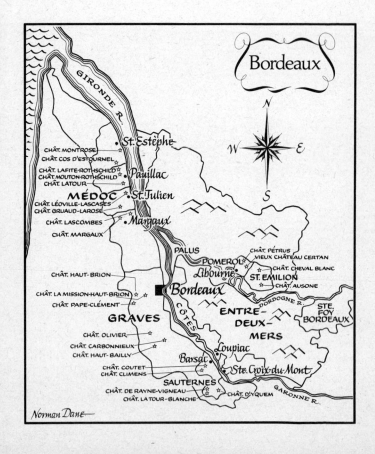

The Bordeaux region is particularly well situated, lying close enough to the Atlantic Ocean to benefit from the moisture, yet inland enough so that the forests in between protect the vineyards from the high ocean winds and excessive moisture. The entire region is laced with tributaries of its three main rivers, which provide ideal drainage. This, together with the mineral-rich subsoil and gravelly topsoil, combines to make Bordeaux an ideal vineyard area. In contrast to Burgundy, many varieties of grapes combine to make the excellence of Bordeaux wines. The four important red-wine varieties are the Cabernet Sauvignon, the Cabernet Franc, the Merlot and the Malbec. The two important white wine grapes are the Sauvignon Blanc and the Sémillon.

The most important district is the Médoc, which lies on the left bank of the Gironde River, extending south for some forty-five miles from the mouth of the river almost to the city of Bordeaux. The northernmost and smallest area is designated simply Médoc. None of these wines are classified above *Cru Bourgeois,* but nevertheless many of them are very creditable Clarets.

The larger area, which lies to the south and is more inland, is designated the Haut-Médoc, which has the largest concentration of fine red wines in the world. The entire Haut-Médoc is divided into fifty-three individual parishes, of which the four most important are St. Estèphe, Pauillac, St. Julien and Margaux. Since these four parishes contain all the important classified growths of the Haut-Médoc, it is best to describe each of these parishes separately, along with their principal classified châteaux, and then continue with the other districts.

ST. ESTEPHE

St. Estèphe is the northernmost of these important parishes. It boasts two important classified second growths, Château Cos d'Estournel and Château Montrose, plus three other classified growths—Château

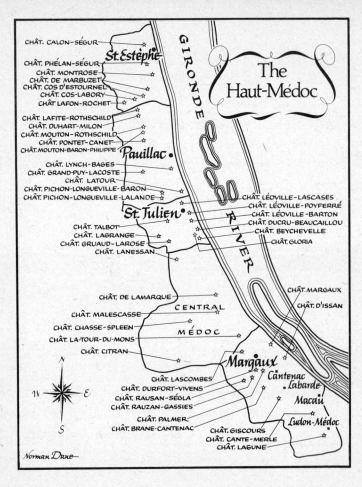

CHÂT. CALON-SÉGUR
St. Estèphe
CHÂT. PHÉLAN-SÉGUR
CHÂT. MONTROSE
CHÂT. DE MARBUZET
CHÂT. COS D'ESTOURNEL
CHÂT. COS-LABORY
CHÂT. LAFON-ROCHET

CHÂT. LAFITE-ROTHSCHILD
CHÂT. DUHART-MILON
CHÂT. MOUTON-ROTHSCHILD
CHÂT. PONTET-CANET
CHÂT. MOUTON-BARON-PHILIPPE
Pauillac

CHÂT. LYNCH-BAGES
CHÂT. GRAND-PUY-LACOSTE
CHÂT. LATOUR
CHÂT. PICHON-LONGUEVILLE-BARON
CHÂT. PICHON-LONGUEVILLE-LALANDE

GIRONDE

RIVER

The Haut-Médoc

CHÂT. LÉOVILLE-LASCASES
CHÂT. LÉOVILLE-POYFERRÉ
CHÂT. LÉOVILLE-BARTON
CHÂT. DUCRU-BEAUCAILLOU
CHÂT. BEYCHEVELLE
CHÂT. GLORIA

St. Julien

CHÂT. TALBOT
CHÂT. LAGRANGE
CHÂT. GRUAUD-LAROSE
CHÂT. LANESSAN

CHÂT. DE LAMARQUE
CENTRAL
MÉDOC
CHÂT. MALESCASSE
CHÂT. CHASSE-SPLEEN
CHÂT. LA-TOUR-DU-MONS
CHÂT. CITRAN

CHÂT. MARGAUX
CHÂT. D'ISSAN

Margaux
Cantenac
Labarde
Macau
Ludon-Médoc

CHÂT. LASCOMBES
CHÂT. DURFORT-VIVENS
CHÂT. RAUSAN-SÉGLA
CHÂT. RAUZAN-GASSIES
CHÂT. PALMER
CHÂT. BRANE-CANTENAC
CHÂT. GISCOURS
CHÂT. CANTE-MERLE
CHÂT. LAGUNE

N
W E
S

Norman Dane

Calon-Ségur (third), Château Lafon-Rochet (fourth) and Château Cos-Labory (fifth)—plus the very creditable wines of Château de Marbuzet and Château Phélan-Ségur.

Château Cos d'Estournel is the most renowned of the classified second growths and the leading classified growth of St. Estèphe. Its famous vineyard lies just beside the venerable Château Lafite-Rothschild, separated only by the little stream that drains both vineyards and forms the boundary between the parishes of St. Estèphe and Pauillac.

Louis Gaspard d'Estournel created this great vineyard in the early 1830s. He was an absurdly extravagant man, whose dream was to crown the nobility of his vineyard with an equally imposing château. Unfortunately, he was unable to finish the château; only the spectacularly delightful Burmese facade, complete with bell tower and pagodas, was built with the d'Estournel coat of arms surmounting the imposing gateway arch. As a result, this great vineyard is familiarly referred to simply as Cos d'Estournel, without the "Château," because, in fact, there is still no château. Two great doors of magnificently carved teak studded with brass—a gift to M. d'Estournel from the sultan of Zanzibar—open directly on to the *chai* in which the famous Claret matures in its casks.

Over the years, the unusual facade of Cos has captured the fancy of several celebrated writers. Stendhal wrote of its architectural elegance and gaiety, Dupouy marveled at its resemblance to a Chinese fairy-tale palace, and the Bordeaux poet Edouard Biarnez glorified this renowned château when he wrote:

There stands Cos d'Estournel
Equal to the greatest growths of Gironde
In all its glory, shining through the world.

This is indeed the world fame of Château Cos d'Estournel, whose wines combine body and delicacy, vigor and generosity with a harmonious bouquet and a balanced taste. As testimony of its superiority, it is said that the heads of Lafite, right next door, when they do not drink their own noble wine, favor Cos d'Estournel. Apparently, in their sophisticated judgment, Cos combines the great qualities of the "big four" of the Médoc—firm, full and big, like Mouton and Latour, yet with the classic finesse of Lafite and Margaux. Today Château Cos d'Estournel is the property of the Domaines Prats, who are also the proprietors of a number of other fine châteaux in St. Estèphe, St. Emilion and Pomerol.

The other classified second growth is Château Montrose, which also makes big, strong, long-lasting wines with a deep color. The château itself is very typical of the old-style wine estate, where special pains have been taken to maintain the traditions of old Bordeaux.

The only third growth is Château Calon-Ségur, which has the reputation for consistently good quality, rather than for flashes of brilliance. The name is derived from the Comte de Ségur, who also owned Château Phélan-Ségur, a Cru Bourgeois Exceptionelle.

Also included in St. Estèphe is Château Lafon-Rochet, a classified fourth growth, which recently gained distinction when its new owner, M. Testeron, completely rebuilt the château. The only fifth growth is Château Cos-Labory. Also worthy of mention is the elegant and distinguished Château de Marbuzet, owned by the Prats of Cos d'Estournel, which lies close by.

PAUILLAC

Pauillac is considered the "richest" parish of the

Haut-Médoc, because it boasts three of the "big five" Clarets—Château Lafite-Rothschild, Château Latour and Château Mouton-Rothschild. In addition, within Pauillac there are two second growths, one fourth growth and nine fifth growths.

The most renowned first growth is Château Lafite-Rothschild. Its history dates back to the Middle Ages when it was owned by the Lafite family, whose wines earned them the reputation of "princes of the vineyards." The property is one of the largest in Médoc, and after changing hands many times, it was sold to Baron James de Rothschild in 1868, whose heirs still own it today.

Ranking right beside Lafite is Château Latour, the other first growth of Pauillac, whose vineyard was created in 1680 and hence is one of the oldest in Médoc. The name Latour derives from the medieval tower that still stands on the property as the only remains of the castle of St. Lambert, which was destroyed when the English were driven out of Gascony.

Château Mouton-Rothschild, the third of the "big five," has a proud history, with many illustrious owners, going as far back as the 14th century. Until recently it was considered in a special category because in 1855 it was classified as the leading second growth, but it has now been reclassified as a first growth.

Perhaps its original classification as a second growth is traceable to the sale of the château in 1853 to the Baron Nathan de Rothschild of the English branch, who lived in London and who apparently was unable to represent himself at the 1855 classification. When the results of the classification reached the baron, in the true Rothschild tradition he proclaimed this challenging motto: *Premier ne puis, second ne daigne, Mouton suis* ("First I cannot be, second I do not deign to be, Mouton I am").

This challenge was rather prophetic, because Château Mouton-Rothschild was proudly vindicated when, ahead of the four classified first growths, it alone was awarded the *Grand Prix Diplome* at the XIII Exposition of Bordeaux. Château Mouton-Rothschild also has a reputation as being the showplace of all Médoc— with its magnificent, exquisitely furnished château, its gently lit cellars, where the *barriques* are in perfect alignment, and the little museum built by the present baron to house works of art associated with wine.

The two second growths of Pauillac are Château Pichon-Longueville and Château Pichon-Lalande. These two fine vineyards were once one huge property, but now they are separate châteaux, facing each other across the road and vying constantly for superiority. The single fourth growth is Château Duhart-Milon, which is owned by the Rothschilds of Château Lafite and whose wines thus benefit from their great skill and experience. In much the same vein, the other Rothschilds own Château Mouton-Baron-Philippe, which really rates higher than its classification as a fifth growth because of the finesse its wines have attained under the expertise of the Mouton-Rothschilds.

Among the fifth growths, Château Pontet-Canet is the best known, and it also has one of the largest productions of all the classified growths in the Haut-Médoc. On a par with it is the equally respected Château Lynch-Bages, whose wines are quite full-bodied with a distinctive flowery bouquet. Another fifth growth that has developed a fine reputation is Château Grand-Puy-Lacoste, whose large vineyards surround its solidly traditional château, which is situated almost in the center of Pauillac.

ST. JULIEN

The somewhat smaller parish of St. Julien has none of the great first growths but more than makes up for it with its five second growths, two third growths and four fourth growths. The most outstanding estate is Léoville, which was once one of the largest in Médoc, before it was divided into three separate Léoville châteaux—Las Cases, Poyferré and Barton, all of which produce excellent wines. Almost in the same class is Château Langoa, a classified third growth owned by the Bartons of Léoville-Barton.

The two other classified second growths are Château Gruaud-Larose and Château Ducru-Beaucaillou. Château Gloria is right next door, and although classified only as a *Cru Bourgeois*, its wines have developed a fine reputation. Also worthy of mention are Château Talbot, a classified fourth growth, which has earned a deserved renown for its typically smooth St. Julien style, and Château Beychevelle, also a fourth growth, which has earned a reputation for its elegance.

Between St. Julien and Margaux to the south is the area known as the Central Médoc, which in a way acts as a bridge between these two important parishes. While there are no classified growths in the Central Médoc, its importance stems from its large production of very sound quality wine, which, when blended with some of the lesser wines of Margaux and St. Julien, is labeled simply "Médoc." Several of the châteaux have developed very fine reputations. Of particular merit are Château Lanessan, a *Cru Bourgeois,* Château Chasse-Spleen, a *Cru Exceptionnel,* and Château La-Tour-du-Mons, one of the best known of the *Crus Bourgeois.*

MARGAUX

The southernmost parish of the Haut-Médoc is Margaux, which many believe produces the finest Clarets of all. A good number of its great châteaux are grouped closely around the town of Margaux. The neighboring parishes of Cantenac and Labarde are also entitled to the *Appellation Margaux Contrôlée,* thereby giving Margaux the largest number of classified growths in the Haut-Médoc—one first growth, five second growths, ten third growths, three fourth growths and one fifth growth; twenty classified growths in all.

The neoclassical style of Château Margaux fits the elegant nobility of its great wine, the fourth of the classified first growths of 1855. Château Margaux was built in the 12th century by the powerful Albret family, and later the entire property belonged to King Edward III, when it was called Château de la Mothe. It was then a fortified castle, entirely surrounded by a wide moat, and the château itself was connected by a series of canals to the Gironde River so that boats could sail right up to its gates. Many of the vineyards were planted during the middle of the 18th century by its then owner, Monsieur de Fumel, who, as the military commander of Bordeaux and a staunch supporter of Lafayette, arranged for his embarkation to America. The present owner is Pierre Ginestet, the grand chancellor of the Bordeaux Wine Academy.

The parish of Margaux also boasts five second growths, including Château Durfort-Vivens, which formerly consisted of two separate properties; Château Lascombes; the well-known pair of Château Rausan-Ségla and Château Rauzan-Gassies, which together once made up the big Rauzan estate; and Château Brane-Cantenac. In addition to these, there are ten third growths, of which the most important are Château Palmer, which has achieved the best reputation, and Château d'Issan, which is known for its magnificent 17th-century fortified château.

ST. EMILION

On the other side of the Gironde, on the right bank of its tributary the Dordogne River, is the medieval town of St. Emilion, whose wines, even in the earliest days, rivaled the great red Graves. They were known then, as they are today, for their rich body, beautiful color and full bouquet, which explains why

they are often called "the Burgundies of Bordeaux." Even though they have more body, the wines of St. Emilion mature somewhat sooner than the great wines of the Médoc, which certainly has contributed to their popularity.

In 1955 the classification of the châteaux of St. Emilion designated twelve first great classified growths and sixty-three great classified growths and, in addition, singled out Château Ausone and Château Cheval Blanc as being particularly spectacular among the first great classified growths.

Château Ausone is generally considered the most famous château of St. Emilion, and if price can be any guide, it certainly ranks with the classified first growths of the Médoc. The origin of the name dates back to Ausonius, the great Roman poet, who was born in Burdigalia (Bordeaux) and who retired to this estate after returning from Rome in 383. One of the rarities of Château Ausone is that a number of its vines were able to survive the phylloxera and therefore are among the oldest vines in Bordeaux. At the eastern end of St. Emilion is the other spectacular first great classified growth, Château Cheval Blanc, which, together with Château Ausone, ranks as the finest of St. Emilion.

Among the other first great classified growths, the most distinguished are Château Figeac and Château La Tour-du-Pin-Figeac, both of which are almost equal to the nearby Château Cheval Blanc. In addition, in this first classification are Château Canon, Château Pavie and Château Magdelaine—all of which have a fine reputation. Included in the great classified growths are the outstanding Château Troplong-Mondot, Château La Dominique and Château Fonroque. Among the principal other growths, Château Petit-Figeac and Château La Fleur-Pourret have both earned very deserved reputations for their reliably fine quality.

POMEROL

The fourth great red wine area is Pomerol, which is the smallest and also the most recently recognized. While St. Emilion and Pomerol lie side by side, Pomerol was not granted the privilege of the English trading rights by Richard the Lionhearted because it had

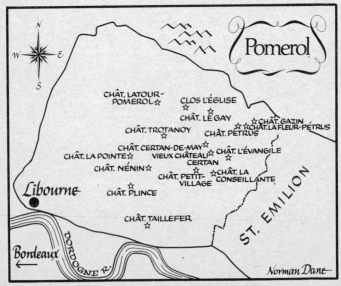

always remained loyal to the king of France. As a result, the *vignerons* of Pomerol did not enjoy the expansion of the château wine trade with England, and therefore they remained as small vineyard farmers.

This tradition still exists in Pomerol, where the châteaux do not have the Bordeaux magnificence, but in the last thirty years their fine wines have been properly discovered and appreciated. It is interesting to note that in both Pomerol and St. Emilion the leading grape is not the Cabernet Sauvignon, but rather the Merlot, which gives to these wines the beautiful combination of richness, softness and fruitiness.

Lacking the status of an official classification, the vintners of Pomerol set up their own "unofficial" classification, which has been commercially recognized by the Bordeaux Wine Trade. Château Pétrus and Vieux-Château-Certan are recognized as the two outstanding vineyards of Pomerol and are almost on a par with the classified first growths of the Médoc. Vieux-Château-Certan is not only one of the finest vineyards in Pomerol but also one of the few that boasts a beautiful château.

Following closely behind are some fine vineyards, of which the most outstanding are Château Petit-Village, Château Certan-de-May, Château La Fleur-Pétrus, Château Gazin and Château Latour-Pomerol. They have all earned for themselves a most deserved reputation as some of the finest châteaux in Pomerol.

GRAVES

The Graves region extends south from the Médoc for about thirty-five miles on the left bank of the river, which now becomes the Garonne. The city of Bordeaux lies in the very northern part, and, historically, many of the finest red Graves were grown on the outskirts of the city, as many still are today. When the people of Bordeaux first devoted themselves to winemaking, the vineyards quite naturally were planted right around the little town of Bordeaux. By the 17th century, the red wines of the Graves had earned a reputation as the finest of all Bordeaux Clarets.

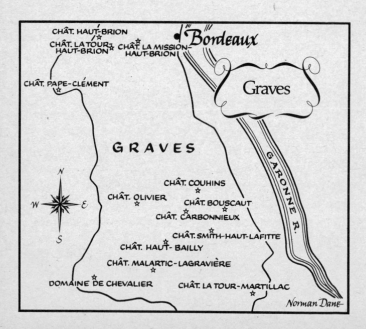

As the city expanded, many of the fine vineyards disappeared, and after the phylloxera scourge, most of the vineyards in the south were replanted with the Sauvignon Blanc and the Sémillon grapes, so that today the production of white Graves is about three times that of red. The four principal parishes in Graves are Pessac, Talence, Léognan and Martillac. Although there are no sharply defined areas for red and white wines, as a general rule the fine red Graves are in the north with the white Graves in the south. Therefore, the best description of the Graves region is by type of wine.

The "king of the red Graves," and the only Graves to be included in the classification of 1855, is the first growth Château Haut-Brion, which is just on the outskirts of Bordeaux. The name dates back to the lordship of Brion, one of whose lords was the mayor of Bordeaux in 1525, but the name was changed to Haut-Brion when the lordship was dissolved during the French Revolution. This great château has changed hands many times and is now owned by Clarence Dillon, the well-known American financier.

In 1953 the official classification of red Graves designated thirteen châteaux as classified growths, with no separation as to first, second, etc. The most famous of these is Château Pape-Clément, which was created in 1300 by Bertrand de Goth, the archbishop of Bordeaux who later became Pope Clement V, famed for having established the papacy at Avignon. The vineyard was passed on to the next archbishop, who then changed the name to Château Pape-Clément, and as such it surely must be one of the oldest in Bordeaux.

Château Haut-Bailly is regarded as the next in importance and is somewhat unusual, since it is located in the southern parish of Léognan, which generally produces only white wines. Almost equal in stature is Château La Mission-Haut-Brion, in the parish of Talence, almost within the city limits of Bordeaux itself. The name and origin of this château date back to its founding by the Order of St. Vincent de Paul in the 17th century, when the vineyard was planted to make wine for the princes of the Church.

The term *Graves* is recognized today as referring to semidry white wines, which American vintners have tried to emulate with the rather contradictory name of "dry Sauternes." The important Graves are all produced in the southern part of the Graves region and particularly in Léognan.

The classification of 1953 also designated eight white Graves as classified growths. One of the best known is Château Olivier, whose medieval fortresslike château dates back to the 11th century, when it was the hunting lodge of Edward, the Black Prince. Equally well known is the nearby Château Carbonnieux, whose castle was built around 1380. From 1519 to 1741, the property belonged to the Benedictine monks of St. Croix, who were among the first to cultivate white wines in this region. They labeled their wine "Carbonnieux" (carbonated water) to disguise it, which enabled them to ship it to

Turkey, where wine was forbidden, to be used as sacramental wine. Also highly regarded is the elegant Château Piron, which has been owned by the Boyreau family for nearly 300 years.

SAUTERNES

Down near the southern tip of the Graves is the distinctive region of Sauternes, which includes the five communes of Sauternes, Farques, Bommes, Preinac and Barsac. (The latter has the alternative of calling its wines either Sauternes or Barsac.) The specialty of Sauternes is its richly luscious and highly perfumed white wine, which is approached only by the *Trockenbeerenauslese* of Germany, the result of a similar late-harvesting technique.

According to legend, this special harvesting technique developed quite by accident. The story goes that the owner of Château Yquem was delayed on a hunting trip and could only return four weeks after the vintage should have been held. Although the grapes had become shriveled and had developed a curious mold, the vintage was held nevertheless. To everyone's surprise, the wine was magnificent—rich, luscious and perfumed—quite unlike anything that had ever been made before. The French call this dried-out, overripe condition *pourriture noble*, which means "noble rot"—the mold causes the juice to evaporate in the autumn sun, leaving a greater concentration of sugar. The special mold is *botrytis cinerea*, which also gives the wine its special bouquet. In its highest refinement, this harvesting technique involves picking over the vineyard as many as seven or eight times, each time selecting only those grapes that are perfectly overripe. Only the wealthiest châteaux can afford this expensive technique, which involves costly labor and produces only one-third the normal yield.

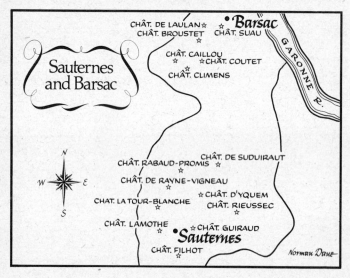

Sauternes were included in the classification of 1855, wherein Château d'Yquem was singled out as the only superior first growth. In addition, eleven châteaux were classified as first growths and thirteen were classified as second growths. As the only superior first growth, Château d'Yquem is certainly in a class by itself.

The celebrated medieval Château Yquem was originally the property of Pierre Ayquem, who was the wine merchant to Edward II in the 14th century. In 1785 the property passed through marriage to the Marquis de Lur-Saluces, whose heirs are still the proud proprietors. The vineyards surrounding Château Yquem have been so meticulously planted and maintained that their perfection is like a painting, quite equal to the perfection of Château d'Yquem in the glass.

Among the eleven châteaux classified as first growths, several are particularly outstanding and often approach the magnificence of Château d'Yquem. The best known of these is Château La Tour-Blanche, which was donated to the state in 1910 by its proprietor, Monsieur Osiris, with the proviso that the state operate the château as a free school of viticulture, supported by the proceeds of the vineyards. Today the school is operated by the Ministry of Agriculture under a board of directors composed of prominent Bordeaux wine-growers and financiers.

The next most prominent growth is Château de Rayne-Vigneau, which for generations has been the property of the Vicomtes de Pontac. As evidence of its excellence, it was awarded gold medals in the World Expositions in 1867 and 1878 and again in the French Expositions in 1925 and 1926. Two other important first growths are Château Rieussec and Château Guiraud, both of which are only a mile away from Château Yquem. Then, in the parish of Barsac, there are two other important first growths—the well-known vineyards of Château Climens and Château Coutet, both of whose wines have somewhat more body but still the same lusciousness of the finest Sauternes. Also in Barsac is the very elegant Château de Laulan, whose delightful wines have earned a very deserved reputation.

OTHER DISTRICTS

In addition to the five major districts of Bordeaux, on the eastern side of the Gironde and Garonne rivers are found the districts of Côtes de Blaye, Côtes de Bourg, Entre-deux-Mers and Premières Côtes de Bordeaux. These regions are large-producing areas, whose wines are most creditable and, at the same time, usually less expensive. Interestingly enough, the somewhat smaller districts of Blaye and Bourg were actually exporting their wines long before the great Médoc district was even planted. Their wines became overshadowed by the mighty Médoc, but these districts are again coming into prominence because of the great shortage of reasonably priced wines.

The *Côtes de Blaye* is a rather large district that specializes in dry, modestly priced white wines. Only a few châteaux have gained particular renown, of which the most important are Château Barbé and Château Segonzac. The *Côtes de Bourg* is a somewhat smaller district on the right bank of the Dordogne River, directly facing Margaux on the other side. A number of châteaux have gained some renown for their very creditable red wines, of which the best known are Château du Bousquet, Château Falfas and Château Brivazac.

Entre-deux-Mers is the largest of all of these districts, producing a large quantity of somewhat fruity white wine, all of which is both modestly priced and of rather modest quality. The *Premières Côtes de Bordeaux* is a smaller district that lies between the Garonne River and Entre-deux-Mers. It produces a number of rather distinguished red wines, among which are Château Plassans, Château de Haux and Château La Peyruche, which have earned for themselves a fine reputation as *petits châteaux*.

The Wines of Alsace

Alsace has always been the buffer province of northeastern France, lying between the Rhine River on the east and the Vosges Mountains on the west and extending south from Strasbourg to the Swiss border. Historically, its strategic importance stems from the fact that Alsace has always commanded the great paths of commerce and communication—the Rhine River flowing to the north, the Sauverne Pass to the west and the Burgundian Gate to the south. Its description as a buffer province could not be more appropriate, since throughout history Alsace has been continually handed back and forth between France and Germany.

In 58 B.C., when Caesar sent his Roman legions into Alsace to drive out the German chief Ariovistus, the Romans built their fortified camp at Argentoratum, which the Franks later renamed Strasbourg ("Town of the Crossways") when they captured the whole area in the fifth century A.D. In 923, as a gesture of homage to Louis the German during the famous "Strasbourg Oaths," Charles the Bold of Burgundy formally deeded the town of Strasbourg to the German kingdom, of which it remained a part until 1681 when King Louis XIV, heeding the Alsatians' pleas for help, courageously seized Alsace for France.

After the Alsatians were rescued from German

domination in 1681, they became forever fervently French in spirit, and during the French Revolution no other province of France took up the fight more zealously. The Alsatians' patriotic spirit is best symbolized by the famous French marching song that was composed in 1792 by Rouget de Lisle, a young French captain stationed at Strasbourg. His marching song quickly became known throughout France as "La Marseillaise," and it is still the French national anthem. Alsace remained French until 1871 when Strasbourg surrendered to the conquering Germans during the Franco-Prussian War. Alsace was then under German rule until it was recaptured by France in 1918, after the defeat of Kaiser Wilhelm II. Since then, Alsace has remained a province of France except for the few years during World War II when it was occupied by the Nazis.

Alsace's political history has continually affected its wines and is completely responsible for their singularity today. The unusual climate of the narrow vineyard strip along the base of the Vosges Mountains fostered native grapes, which the Gauls apparently just ate. When the Romans came, they cultivated the vine to abundance and the wines from Alsace soon became hard competition for the native Italian wines. By the Middle Ages, the wines of Aussay, as Alsace was then known, were already famous—their fame aided greatly by the fact that they could be shipped so easily to the outside world on the natural waterway of the Rhine River.

When the Germans conquered Alsace in 1871, they decided to make Alsace an integral part of Germany and therefore decreed that all Alsatian wines had to be shipped in bulk to Germany, where they were blended with the German Rhines and Moselles. At the same time, the Alsatian vintners were required to produce for quantity and not for quality, in order to increase the total "German" production. As a result, from 1871 until 1914 Alsatian wines lost not only their quality image but also their international identity. Then came World

War I and Alsace joyfully became French again; yet from a wine point of view, they were faced with disaster. The Alsatian vintner suddenly had to compete against the gamut of all other French wines, and instead of having quality-producing vines, he could produce only volume.

Undoubtedly fortified by the courage born out of centuries of turmoil, the Alsatians made the imaginative decision to replant their vineyards and dedicate themselves to the exclusive production of fine-quality, distinctive wines. As testimony to their success, the French foreign minister wrote: "Beginning in 1919, a grand battle was launched which has been magnificently won —the battle for quality. Improvement of vine types and the perfection of methods of vinification have given Alsatian wines a luster that lets them enter the privileged circle of great French wines."

ALSACE

The vineyard region of Alsace is only about sixty miles long and never more than a mile or two wide, but its uniqueness lies in its being blessed with an unusual climate. Wine grapes usually flourish best in warm climates, and only in very few favored spots do they grow so far north. In Alsace, the vineyards lie in the foothills of the Vosges Mountains and are thus sheltered by the high mountains rising steeply behind. The vineyards face south and east, so that they catch a maximum amount of sun. Because of the peculiarities of the climate, in the actual vineyard area there is less than one-third the rainfall of the adjoining plain, and at the same time there are fifty more days of sunshine each year.

Even though the Alsatian vineyards are protected by their unique climate, the fact that Alsace is still rather far north is also beneficial. Colder weather can often make for better wine because the grape matures more slowly, which increases its fruitiness. It also seems to be a quirk of nature that fine wines the world over are often the result of the struggle of the vine against nature.

In 1919, when the Alsatian vintners were faced with rebuilding their vineyards, they decided their future lay in promoting the intense fruitiness of their wines, providing that they could develop wine-making methods that would ensure maximum preservation of freshness and fruitiness right to the glass. They replanted their

vines and trained them to grow on parallel wires to encourage their growth to six or seven feet. This struggle to reach the sun increased both the yield and the fruitiness and at the same time permitted cleaner cultivation, which exposed the vines to the maximum amount of sunlight and air, thus promoting their growth and producing more fully ripened grapes. The key to understanding the Alsatian wine-making process lies in realizing that fruitiness and freshness are both highly perishable and that therefore the wine must always be protected from the air. Single racking, whereby the wine is handled and exposed to the air as little as possible, is the keystone of the Alsatian process and is peculiar only to Alsace.

In Alsace, all grapes are collected, transferred and pressed in meticulously clean receptacles so that they carry the least possible amount of foreign matter. A new "inner tube" type of press is used almost exclusively because it permits extremely delicate control. This press is a long, perforated drum into which the grapes are dumped, and down the center runs a rubber sleeve, which is something like an inner tube stretched lengthwise. As the inner tube is inflated, it expands slowly and crushes the grapes against the cylinder sides, forcing the juice to run out through the perforations. Because such care has been taken to eliminate foreign matter, the juice falls clear in twenty-four to forty-eight hours and is then transferred into tremendous wooden casks where it remains until bottling. Wine of the same single grape variety and from the same vineyard sector is usually made in the same large cask every year, which is another special feature of Alsatian wine-making.

Because of the cold weather and because all impurities have been excluded except the pure native grape yeasts, the juice begins to ferment only after five or six days. When fermentation stops about thirty days later, the cask is filled to the brim and tightly closed so that the wine is shut off completely from the air. Tremendous oval casks are used because they permit less air to reach the wine through the pores of the wood.

The secret of the Alsatian wine-maker is the direct road his grapes follow from vine to bottle—clean gathering, immediate pressing, minimum handling, aeration by single racking, final filtering and then bottling. The whole process is simple and completely direct. Bottling takes place early, around eight months after the vintage, and because of these immaculate vinification methods, Alsatian wines maintain their freshness and fruitiness for upward of twelve years. As one more precaution, Alsatian wine corks are always extra long, to further protect the precious fruitiness of the wine.

Alsatian wines are also unique in that they are generally named for the grape variety. There are exceptions, of course, such as the wines from the great vineyards of Clos Gaensbroennel in Barr and Clos Sainte-Odile in Obernai, which are two of the most spectacular Alsatian wines.

Basically, the most important varieties of Alsatian wine are:

Riesling—An elegant and distinguished wine, delicate and fragrant, with a fine and subtle bouquet. Riesling is considered the unquestioned king of Alsatian wines.

Gewürztraminer—A superior quality of Traminer (*Gewürz* means "spice" in German). A very rich, fruity, full-bodied wine with a deep, flowery bouquet.

Traminer—Basically similar, yet of a lesser quality, to Gewürztraminer.

Sylvaner—A lighter but still fruity wine that is always quite delightful.

There is one further word about the history of Alsatian wines that particularly concerns the United States. Alsatian wines lost their identity from 1871 to 1918, when all Alsatian wines were blended with German wines. Then the United States had Prohibition, from 1921 to 1933. Therefore, no Alsatian wines were available in the United States from 1871 to 1933, which means that almost three generations of Americans never saw a bottle of Alsatian wine. Notwithstanding the wine explosion, it is obvious that the lack of popularity of Alsatian wines in this country is completely due to their lack of exposure. It remains only for us to discover their greatness.

The Loire Valley

The Loire is the longest river in France. After its source in the Massif Central, it flows gently westward from Pouilly-sur-Loire to Nantes, where it empties into the Atlantic Ocean. The Loire Valley extends some 350 miles, with a vineyard area of about 500,000 acres, making it France's second largest wine-producing area. Basically, the valley is divided into four rather sepa-

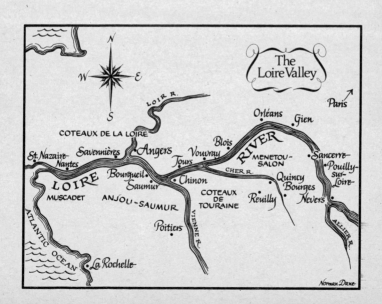

rate regions, which, from inland toward the Atlantic, are the Central Region, the Coteaux de Touraine, Anjou-Saumur and Muscadet. Since the important wines of each region are somewhat different, it is best to discuss each region separately.

THE CENTRAL REGION

The Central Region, which centers around the towns of Pouilly-sur-Loire on the right bank of the river and Sancerre on the left bank, is the first of the important wine regions of the Loire Valley. During the 15th century, the Cistercian monks founded an abbey near Quincy and brought with them from Bordeaux some cuttings of the Sauvignon Blanc, which unexpectedly developed rather differently on the Loire. The grape became known as the Blanc Fumé, because of a peculiar bluish-gray mistlike dust that settles on the grapes and blows in the air during the vintage. The Blanc Fumé produces a delightfully dry, yet fruity, white wine, which is becoming very popular with all who have discovered it.

The Blanc Fumé is planted in the four neighboring towns of Pouilly-sur-Loire, Sancerre, Quincy and Reuilly. The wines from the latter three communes use their own appellations, while those from Pouilly-sur-Loire have two appellations. When the wines of Pouilly-sur-Loire are from the Blanc Fumé, they are sold as "Pouilly-Fumé," but when they are made from the Chasselas grape, they must be sold as "Pouilly-sur-Loire," which has less body and bouquet and is best when drunk quite young. As a comparison, the wines of Sancerre are more mellow than Pouilly-Fumé, while those of Quincy are a little drier.

COTEAUX DE TOURAINE

The Coteaux de Touraine is a wide area on both banks of the Loire around the city of Tours. The hillsides around Tours were first planted with vines around the 14th century and are some of the oldest vineyards in the Loire Valley. This region produces red, white and rosé wines, using for the white wines the Pineau de la Loire and the Sauvignon Blanc, and for the red the Cabernet Franc and the Gamay.

Touraine is best known for the very popular Vouvray, whose vineyards surround the little village of Vouvray, just to the northeast of Tours. Vouvray can be a delightfully light and cheerful wine that often has a slight *pétillance*. When the wine develops too much acidity, then it is perfect for making into Sparkling Vouvray by the traditional *méthode champenoise*.

Farther down the Loire, around the town of Chinon on the left bank and around the town of Bourgueil on the right, there are two small regions that produce rather distinguished red wines from the Cabernet Franc, both of which are fruity and delicate and somewhat similar. Bourgueil, if anything, has a bit more freshness, while Chinon is slightly more mellow.

ANJOU-SAUMUR

The third region, which is the largest-producing of all, is the combined area of Saumur and Anjou. At one time, the wines of Saumur were the most important of this region, but now the production of Anjou, particularly with rosé, is the most prominent. Saumur is now considered part of Anjou, and as such their wines may be sold either as Saumur or Anjou, while the wines of Anjou can be sold only as Anjou.

Sparkling Saumur is the most important production in Saumur, which, as in Vouvray, is made according to the traditional *méthode champenoise*. Saumur has an advantage over Vouvray in being able to use a certain amount of red grapes, which lend additional body and bouquet to its Sparkling Saumur. Langloise-Château and Ackerman-Lawrence are considered the two leading brands of Sparkling Saumur. Both have gained prominence in France as less expensive "champagnes"— slightly lighter in body and a bit more fruity. They compare quite favorably with some of the less distinguished French champagnes, because they are quality sparkling wines that are made by the traditional *méthode champenoise*.

The Anjou region, which is the largest wine-producing area in the Loire, is situated on the southern bank of the Loire and extends from Saumur past Angers. The popularity of Anjou wines dates back to the sixth century, and there is an infinite variety—whites, reds and rosés; dry, semidry, sweet and dessert wines; and both still and sparkling wines. However, in recent years the delightful Anjou rosé has become so popular that its production has been increased substantially. There are no really outstanding Anjou rosés—they are

all light and delightful, with a fresh and fruity bouquet and flavor, and they are generally sold under the generic label of "Rosé d'Anjou."

There are two wines of this region that because of their distinctiveness deserve special mention. At the western end of the Anjou region is the Coteaux du Layon, which is particularly known for luscious white wines, the finest of which come from the small appellation of Quarts-de-Chaume. This interesting name, which means "quarters of Chaume," developed because the proprietor of one of the famous vineyards around the little village of Chaume habitually gave three-quarters of his production to the local people who had helped him tend the vineyards and make the wine. The wines of Quarts-de-Chaume are comparable to Sauternes, with a similar amber color, a luscious flavor and a gentle perfume.

The other rather special wines of Anjou come from the small area of Savennières, which lies just across the Loire River. The wines of Savennières are rather surprising, with their very flowery bouquet yet delicately dry taste—sort of halfway between the delightful white wines of Anjou and the luscious wines of Quarts-de-Chaume.

MUSCADET

The rather large region of Muscadet is at the mouth of the Loire on the small promontory that juts out into the Atlantic. It is the second largest producing area of the Loire Valley and has recently become popular for its delightful, pale yellow Muscadet, with its lightly delicate bouquet and flavor.

The vineyards in this region take their name from the Muscadet grape, which in itself has an interesting history. Exposed to the rigors of the harsh winters of the Atlantic, almost all the original vineyards of the region were destroyed during the severe winter of 1709. Some of the vintners successfully replanted their vineyards with the hardier Muscadet grape from Burgundy, and after the ravages of the phylloxera epidemic, the other vintners followed their example and also replanted with the Muscadet. For many years, Muscadet was considered somewhat second class, which makes its recent popularity all the more exceptional.

The Rhone Valley and Southern France

The region of the Rhone Valley extends south along the Rhone River for some 135 miles, from the ancient city of Vienne, which became a Roman colony around 47 B.C., down to Avignon, which was the Romans' leading city in the province of Gallia Narbonensis. The Rhone region is composed essentially of five sometimes widely separated vineyard areas that have each been designated with their own *Appellation Contrôlée*. Because of the changes in soil and climate that occur along the length of the Rhone Valley, different vine stocks are used, and therefore the wines produced in the separate areas differ quite markedly. While each of the four appellations are both distinctive and different, the larger Côtes du Rhône appellation has become the most important, because of the great popularity of the rather full-bodied and fruity red wines that are sold under the "Côtes du Rhône" appellation.

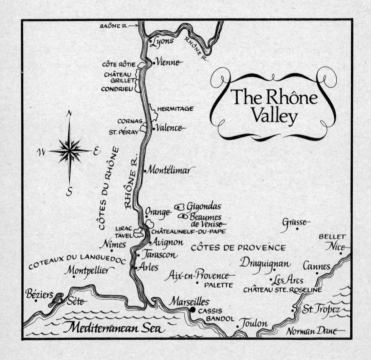

The Rhône Valley

COTE ROTIE

The small vineyard area of Côte Rôtie lies just across the Rhone from Vienne, on a short stretch of very steep hills situated so that they are drenched by the sun—hence the name Côte Rôtie, meaning "roasted slope." Here the classic red Syrah grape produces probably the very best red wines of the Côtes du Rhône, which are very slow to mature but which finally develop a delicacy not unlike that of a fine Burgundy.

CONDRIEU

This area is almost a continuation of the Côte Rôtie, yet it is quite different. Only the white Voignier grape is used, which produces a rather delicate white wine, quite dry, with good body and a flowery bouquet. The most famous of these wines is Château Grillet, whose four-acre estate is the smallest in France to have been accorded its own *Appellation Contrôlée*.

HERMITAGE

According to legend, a returning crusader, Henri Gaspard de Sterimberg, retired here after the wars to live the contemplative life of a hermit. Apparently he brought with him from Persia the first vine cuttings of the Syrah grape and thus established the vineyards that today cover the entire hill of Hermitage. The adjective most descriptive of the wines of Hermitage is "manly." These are big wines that throw a heavy sediment and have great staying power, yet they continue to improve in the bottle. Hermitage definitely ranks among the finest of the Côtes du Rhône.

CHÂTEAUNEUF-DU-PAPE

At the southern end of the Côtes du Rhône, some sixty-five miles south of Hermitage, is Châteauneuf-du-Pape, which lies in the center of the largest vineyard area of the Côtes du Rhône, just north of the ancient city of Avignon.

The origin of the vineyards as we know them today dates back to the 14th century, when Pope Clement V established the papacy at Avignon, starting the so-called Babylonian exile. When Pope Clement V was the archbishop of Bordeaux, he had created the great château later named Pape-Clément, and with his knowledge and interest he quite logically had vineyards planted when he came to Avignon. The new fortress-palace of the popes was started in 1316 by John XXII, who succeeded Clement V, and it was completed in 1370. It was built on a hill that soon became surrounded by vineyards, which were then named after the Châteauneuf-du-Pape—"the new castle of the pope." Only seven years later, Gregory XI returned the papacy to Rome, but the vineyards of Châteauneuf-du-Pape remained and their fame continues to this day.

The wines of Châteauneuf-du-Pape are deep, rich red in color, very full-bodied and robust, with a heady bouquet. Quite curiously, the vines are grown in a "sea of stones," which retain the heat of the day and radiate it to the vines during the cool night. The sandy soil beneath provides perfect drainage, which, together with the stony surface, combines to make Châteauneuf-du-Pape a wine of great finesse and elegance—providing that it's allowed the necessary time to mature. There are a great many estates in Châteauneuf-du-Pape, similar to the châteaux in Bordeaux, but the vast majority of wine is sold under the general appellation of "Châteauneuf-du-Pape."

Of further historical importance is the fact that the French system of *Appellation Contrôlée* was initiated at Châteauneuf-du-Pape, having been developed from the initial proposals made by Baron Le Roy, who was then one of the leading growers. His proposals not only covered the designation of vineyard areas but also specified the basic different grape varieties required for the appellation "Châteauneuf-du-Pape." Just to demonstrate the complexity of Châteauneuf-du-Pape, one famous grower maintains that the perfect formula consists of 20 percent Grenache for warmth and richness, 40 percent Syrah for solidity, 30 percent Picpoul for vinosity and 10 percent Clairette for finesse. This type of mélange is indeed indigenous to Châteauneuf-du-Pape.

TAVEL AND LIRAC

Across the Rhone River, slightly inland and just north of Avignon, are the twin communes of Tavel and Lirac, both of which produce delightful distinctive rosés. Although they are officially classified as wines of the Rhone, the rosés of Tavel and Lirac are often discussed together with the rosés of Provence. Actually, the countryside of Tavel and Lirac is much the same as that of Provence, where the vineyards are also baked, burned and flinty.

Vin rosé is made in virtually every wine-producing region, made in various ways and from various grapes, so that each has its own characteristics. A true rosé gets its color only from genuine methods of vinification.

Since the color pigments are in the skin of the grape, the skin is first broken by crushing or pressing, and the alcohol formed during fermentation extracts the color from the skins. Therefore the fermenting juice is left in contact with the skins until the desired shade of pink is attained. Then the juice alone is drawn off into vats, where it continues to ferment.

In Lirac and Tavel, the latter producing rosés exclusively, the wine is fermented according to an age-old formula that blends together four or more varieties of both red and white grapes, the predominating ones being the Grenache, the Clairette and the Cinsault. Tavels do not have the characteristically orange-pink color so often found in lesser rosés, and they are usually stronger in alcohol, which enables them to travel well.

PROVENCE

The vineyards in Provence are the oldest in France, dating back some 2,500 years to when the first Greek settlers brought vines with them. When the Celts attacked, the Greeks appealed to Rome for help, and Rome helped so successfully that this entire strip and a great deal more fell under Roman rule. The Romans quickly established colonies in the new province, which was called Provincia Romana—hence the name Provence. After centuries of being conquered by one nation after another, Provence finally became an autonomous state in 1450 under the powerful counts of Provence, and shortly thereafter it was united with France.

During all this tumultuous history, the wines of Provence were continually famous and very much in demand. Even during the Middle Ages, Provence wine standards were controlled by legislation, with laws being passed regulating wine production and commerce. The tradition of Provence is exemplified by Les Chevaliers de Méduse, one of the earliest of all bacchanalian orders, which was founded in Provence in 1690.

The vineyards of Provence are planted across the twenty-mile-wide coastal strip, in the valleys from Marseilles over to Monte Carlo and down to the Italian border. Since there were only four small appelations—Palette, Bellet, Bandol and Cassis—the producers did not consider this a satisfactory selection. Consequently, they imposed upon themselves the obligation to submit their wines for analysis, followed by a tasting examination, to determine if the wines were worthy of the *Appellation Contrôlée* "Côtes de Provence." Thus, in 1953, there was adopted the further designation "V.D.Q.S." (*Vins Délimités de Qualité Supérieur*), and only those wines which meet the required standards are granted the V.D.Q.S. designation.

The Côtes de Provence V.D.Q.S. quality control follows the wine from vine to bottle. It begins with restrictions concerning vineyard locations, which are limited to lands having a soil composition determined by a government commission to be ideal for the best vines to be grown. Also, only those grape varieties from specifically authorized vines may be grown, which principally include: the Carignan, which gives the Côtes de Provence rosés their pleasantly dry characteristics; the Grenache, which adds alcoholic content, a light ruby color and a velvety quality; the Cinsault, which provides suppleness and a fruity bouquet; and the Tibouren, which contributes the fruity aroma and fresh finish so distinctive of these rosés.

Not far from the mountain of Melmont, where Julius Caesar sent his administrators to buy some of the then-famous wines, stands the medieval château of Ste. Roseline, which dates back to the 11th century. This castle was formerly the abbey of Celle Roubaud, which was first mentioned in 1038, when the lands were donated to the monks of Saint Victor. In 1200, the abbey and its vineyards were transferred to the nuns of Chartres, and in 1300, when John XXII, the future pope of Avignon, became bishop of Fréjus, he appointed Roseline of Villeneuve the prioress of Celle Roubaud. The great pope never forgot Celle Roubaud, and late in 1334, shortly before his death, he ordered the exhumation of Sainte Roseline de Villeneuve. To this day, her body lies in the little chapel of Ste. Roseline.

The abbey was disbanded during the French Revolution, and after changing hands twice, Château Ste. Roseline was acquired in 1859 by the Baron de Rasque de Laval, whose family still controls the destinies of the domain. It was the present baron who discovered the original records of Les Chevaliers de Méduse, and in 1951 this bacchanalian order was reorganized, after having been disbanded during the French Revolution. The order has many regulatory activities, but the most spectacular ceremony is the autumnal *ban de vendange*. This marks the ideal time to start the vintage, as officially proclaimed by the Chevaliers, resplendant in their full regalia of wine-colored velvet robes, at ceremonies held in the ancient cloister of Château Ste. Roseline. This medieval château is one of the oldest and most renowned estates, and its wine is a true château-bottled *vin rosé de Provence*.

LANGUEDOC, CORBIERES, AND ROUSSILLON

The long sweeping area along the Mediterranean coast, stretching west from Nimes to Narbonne and then inland to Carcassonne, is generally referred to as the Midi. Here the fertile land and sunny climate combine to make this one of the largest wine-producing areas in France. It is usually the case that the greater the production yield, the lesser the quality. This is generally true of the wines of the Midi, but the wines of Languedoc, Corbières and Roussillon are exceptions.

Shortly after the phylloxera scourge, many of the vignerons chose to move south to this more prolific coastal vineyard area, rather than replant their northern vineyards where wine-growing was far more difficult. They brought with them their experience and knowledge of fine wine-making, which they successfully used in planting the better vineyards in the Midi. This is particularly true of the red wines of Languedoc, Corbières and Roussillon, which are considered the quality wines of the Midi and which merit the V.D.Q.S. designation. The red wines of Languedoc are somewhat lighter, while those of Corbières and Roussillon are fuller bodied and fruitier.

The Champagnes of France

At the time of the Roman conquest, vines were already being cultivated in the valley of the Marne. In A.D. 92 Emperor Domitian ordered all vines in Gaul destroyed, especially those in Champagne, so that the wines of Champagne would not become a serious rival to the wines of Italy. Two centuries later, Emperor Probus abolished this strict decree, and according to legend, the people of Champagne then built the triumphal arch of the Porte Mars at Reims to honor him.

However, in those days and in succeeding centuries, the wines of Champagne were still wines. It wasn't until the latter part of the 17th century that, according to legend, the pious Benedictine monk Dom Pérignon, who was then the head cellarer of the abbey of Hautvillers near Epernay, first put bubbles into the wine and gave us champagne as we know it today. Dom Pérignon was also the first to use the bark of the cork tree as a stopper, thereby retaining the sparkle for a much longer period.

By French law, champagne is defined as being a sparkling white wine produced by a secondary fermentation in the bottle and using solely grapes grown in a delimited geographical area, which is roughly equivalent to the old duchy of Champagne. The Champagne region, which is the most northerly wine-producing area of France, lies about seventy-five miles east of Paris, mainly in the department of the Marne. To the east is Alsace, and to the south is Burgundy, with the Marne River forming an important line of division. North of

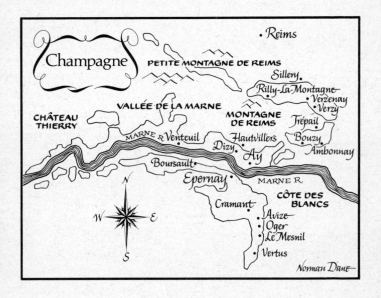

the Marne, around the towns of Ay and Hautvillers and in the Montagne de Reims section, mainly black grapes are grown. South of the Marne lies the Côte des Blancs, where mainly white grapes are grown around the towns of Cramant, Avize, Le Mesnil and Vertus. Pinot Chardonnay and Pinot Noir are the two grape varieties used in champagne, but the chalky soil gives the grapes a special quality, so that the wine made from the same Pinot grape used in Burgundy is quite different.

The *méthode champenoise* is the special procedure used in making French champagne. It is so involved and requires such meticulous attention to detail that a step-by-step description provides the best explanation.

THE CHAMPAGNE VINTAGE

*S*ince champagne is a blend of wines made from grapes grown in a number of different vineyards, no vineyard name appears on the label, which makes the shipper's name all-important. While each important shipper owns vineyards in the various districts, his own vineyards do not produce enough grapes, and therefore he buys additional quantities from the smaller vineyard owners.

Vintage operations usually begin around the end of September, when a veritable army of pickers harvests the grapes throughout the region. The picking of the grapes is carried on under strict supervision in order to make certain that only sound and fully ripened grapes are harvested. The pickers place the grapes in baskets, called *paniers,* carried on their backs. When the *paniers* are full, they are taken to the side of the road where experienced sorters cull out any green, overripe or defective grapes. This selection process is called *épluchage* and is practiced only by the great firms in Champagne. The process applies not only to the firms' own vineyards, but particularly to the additional grapes they buy from the small vineyard owners. Thus, right at the very beginning of the process, there is room for considerable differences in quality.

PRESSING THE GRAPES

*T*he grapes are brought to the pressing house in old-fashioned horse carts and then, after each basket has been marked and weighed to determine the exact quantity being pressed, the grapes are loaded onto the large hydraulic presses. One loading is called a *marc,* totaling four tons, and each *marc* produces about 572 gallons of juice, filling thirteen casks of 44 gallons each. Four pressings are made from each *marc:* the *cuvée,* the *première taille,* the *deuxième taille* and the *rebêche.* Of the thirteen casks of juice produced from each *marc,* the first ten constitute the *cuvée* and the balance of three constitutes the *première* and *deuxième taille* and the *rebêche.*

The great champagne firms, who are so prideful of the quality of their wines, use only the *cuvée* and *première taille* pressings, selling off as bulk wine the *deuxième taille* and the *rebêche.* Here again, at this stage of production, there are understandable reasons for the difference in quality and price of various brands of champagne. Quite obviously, it is more expensive to produce champagne from only the first two pressings.

Both black and white grapes are grown in Champagne, but about two-thirds of the grapes are Pinot Noir. However, champagne is nevertheless a white wine, because the fruit of both Pinot Noir and Pinot Chardonnay grapes is white, with the skin containing all the coloring matter. During pressing, the juice is run off immediately so that the skins are not permitted to give their color to the wine.

At this stage of production, there has been no blending, and each cask is carefully marked with the name of the vineyard where the grapes were grown. The casks are not completely filled, and the bung is left open so that the carbon dioxide created during fermentation may escape. After the first violent fermentation, the wine becomes quiet and the bung is driven home so that the wine rests quietly throughout the winter months. Normally, fermentation should continue until all the sugar is fermented out, but in Champagne the cold weather arrests the fermentation prematurely, leaving some of the sugar unfermented, which will later produce the secondary fermentation, the secret of champagne.

BLENDING THE WINES

*I*n the spring, before the fermentation starts anew, the head cellarman and the heads of the firm taste the wines and decide what proportion of different wines will go into the *cuvée* or blend. This is probably the most important and exacting task in the production of champagne. Years of experience are necessary in order to judge how the new wine, barely six months old and not completely fermented, will taste some five years hence.

Once this decision has been made, the new wines are blended in the established proportions in large blending vats where they are thoroughly married. At this point, the wine is given the *dosage de tirage,* which is a small quantity of the finest rock sugar dissolved in old wine, which ensures a uniform secondary fermentation. Then the wine is fined and immediately bottled. The cork is firmly secured in the neck with a heavy metal clip, known as an *agrafe,* which is strong enough to withstand the pressure created by the secondary fermentation in the bottle, which gives the sparkle to champagne.

THE WINE BECOMES SPARKLING

*T*here are various ways of making a sparkling wine, but the traditional *champenoise* method requires secondary fermentation in the bottle. This is the only method that can legally be used in France if the wine is to bear the designation "Champagne." The great advantage to producing the sparkle through secondary fermentation in the bottle is that the sparkle is natural and much finer in texture, and therefore it lasts longer once the bottle is opened. This secondary fermentation works as follows: When the cold weather arrests the

117

fermentation, some unfermented sugar remains in the wine. With the coming of the warmer spring weather, the remaining sugar begins to ferment and is transformed into alcohol and carbon dioxide gas. This secondary fermentation must take place very slowly if fine, light, continuous bubbles, the desirable signs of quality in a great champagne, are to be obtained.

Therefore, the bottling must be completed before the warm spring. The bottles are stored in below-ground cellars, carved out of the natural chalk subsoil of the Champagne district; they remain at a constant temperature of about ten degrees centigrade. The bottles are stored on their sides and are constantly examined for any breakage or leakage, because the pressure developed during secondary fermentation can be as high as 110 pounds per square inch. In the old days, breakage was as high as every other bottle, but today, with improved bottle manufacture and scientific measuring of the sugar content in the wine, this breakage has been reduced to a minimum.

French law requires that the new wine be aged for at least one year from the time it becomes sparkling, but the great champagne firms age their wines from three to six years. Here is another variable in the process of production that has a considerable effect on the quality and price of various brands.

DISGORGING

*D*uring secondary fermentation and aging, a certain amount of natural sediment develops that must be removed so that the wine will be perfectly clear. In other types of wine, sediment is eliminated before bottling by fining and drawing off the clear wine. In champagne, this is a very complicated process, because it must be accomplished *after* bottling.

The sediment that has formed during secondary

fermentation and aging lies along the side of the bottle and must first be gotten down onto the cork before it can be removed. To do this, the bottles are placed cork down in slanting racks called *pupitres*. Over a period of three to four months, an experienced workman rapidly jiggles each bottle every few days, turning it clockwise an eighth turn each time, thus loosening the sediment and causing it to settle down on the cork. Once this process, called *remuage*, is completed, the bottles are placed cork down in wicker cellar baskets and carried to the *salle de dégorgement*.

Here the neck of the bottle is frozen, imprisoning the sediment in a small block of ice. Then comes one of the most ticklish jobs in the whole process, the *dégorgement*—the removal of the cork together with the frozen sediment, done in such a manner that very little effervescence and very little wine escape. A highly skilled workman, wearing a leather apron and often a wire-covered mask to protect his face from an exploding bottle, grasps the bottle. Standing opposite the barrel and protected by a shield, he releases the *agrafe* with a pair of pliers and the cork flies out, taking with it the frozen bit of sediment. He gives the neck of the bottle two or three sharp raps to loosen any remaining sediment, and in doing so, a small amount of wine foams out, which he examines to be sure it has a perfectly clean bouquet. He then hands the bottle to another workman who adds the *liqueur d'expédition* (shipping dosage), which consists of wine from bottles that have been previously disgorged, in order to replace the wine that has escaped. When somewhat sweeter champagne is required for a particular market, the *liqueur d'expédition* also includes a small amount of rock sugar dissolved in old wine, with the amount of sugar depending on the degree of sweetness required.

The *liqueur d'expédition* can also involve another quality differentiation. While the amount of sugar added basically depends on the requirements of the market, the dosage can also indicate the quality of the wine. The finer the wine, the less dosage is needed, while a heavier dosage is often used to disguise lesser-quality wines.

After the dosage, the shipping cork is driven home and secured in place by the wired cap, and then follows a further aging period to let the wine rest from the strain of *dégorgement*. Finally, after five years and all these delicate operations, the wine is ready to be labeled, packed and shipped. At this point, the role of the importer enters as a final determination of quality. Since champagne is the most delicate of all quality wines, it therefore suffers the most from the turmoil of the ocean voyage. Importers of the finer champagnes let the wine rest in warehouses for three or four months before shipping it to the trade. This again is another costly procedure that only the importers of finer champagnes can afford.

THE IMPORTANCE OF BRAND NAMES

*I*n review, it is understandable that the *méthode champenoise* is a long, involved and meticulous process. It is also a very costly one, since it requires an unusual amount of hand labor and a large immobilization of capital. These are the defining variables which make the *méthode champenoise* so demanding:

1. The quality of the grapes used and the care with which they are picked and selected.
2. The use of only the juice of the first two pressings, the *cuvée* and the *première taille,* as opposed to using all four pressings, which gives a 10 percent greater yield.
3. The care and skill with which the wines from various vineyards are blended together.
4. The aging of the wine before disgorging, which

can vary from the legal minimum of one year to a maximum of five to six years.

5. The shipping dosage, which, while dictated by the market requirements, can also be used to disguise a lesser-quality wine.

Many variations in procedure can affect the cost and quality of the final product, all of which account for the variance in quality between individual brands. The brand name is perhaps more important in champagne than in any other wine, because champagne is not the product of any single vineyard but rather is a blended wine produced by a delicate and demanding process.

VINTAGE AND NONVINTAGE WINES

*E*very champagne producer markets both vintage and nonvintage wines. The great champagne firms market as vintage wines only those years that produce superior wines, ones sufficiently well balanced and individualistic to meet their own exacting standards. Vintage wines are the true *drapeau* of the great firms, on which they have built their reputations over the years.

Recently the great firms have expanded the importance of vintage wines by marketing a new category of "super" champagne. These are primarily somewhat older wines, of a special *cuvée,* which are often in a special fancy bottle. The exception is Bollinger R.D., which is distinctively different from Bollinger's current vintage wine. In the *méthode champenoise,* after the dosage has been added following *dégorgement,* the wine does not improve any further in the bottle. In Bollinger, the initials "R.D." stand for *récemment dégorgé,* indicating that the wine has been permitted to age for an additional five years before being disgorged. As a result, Bollinger R.D. is richer, more mature and fuller bodied, yet with the same effervescence of a younger wine—truly a super champagne.

On the other hand, nonvintage wines are a blend of wines produced from grapes grown in various years. When the wines of a given year are not up to "vintage" standards, they are blended with wines of other vintage years, so as to produce the desired well-balanced wine. Since several of the leading champagne firms use only wines of the same high quality, produced under the same high standards as their vintage wines, their nonvintage wines are equally superior in quality, yet with the same taste year after year.

*E*very bottle of champagne bears one of the following designations: "Brut," "Extra Dry," "Sec" or "Demi-Sec," with "Brut" being that shipper's driest wine and "Demi-Sec" his sweetest. In this country, only the designations "Brut" and "Extra Dry" are generally used, while wines labeled "Sec" and "Demi-Sec" are usually found in Latin American countries. These designations are not definitive terms since there are no prescribed standards as to what degree of dryness constitutes a "Brut" champagne or what degree of sweetness constitutes a "Demi-Sec" champagne. Here again, each shipper establishes his own standards for these designations; consequently the "Brut" wine of a given shipper may or may not be drier that the "Extra Dry" wine of another shipper.

 *T*he distinctiveness of the *méthode champenoise* and the uniqueness of the traditions of champagne have been carried through to the champagne bottle—which is special to champagne, in design, in contents and even in name. These are the traditional names and contents of the various sizes of champagne bottles:

Split, baby or nip	6½ fluid ounces
Pint	13 fluid ounces
Bottle or quart	26 fluid ounces
Magnum (2 quarts)	52 fluid ounces
Jeroboam (double magnum)	104 fluid ounces
Rehoboam (6 bottles)	156 fluid ounces
Methuselah (8 bottles)	208 fluid ounces
Salmanazar (12 bottles)	312 fluid ounces
Balthazar (16 bottles)	416 fluid ounces
Nebuchadnezzar (20 bottles)	520 fluid ounces

Only the first five sizes are generally sold commercially, which means that the jeroboam is normally the largest size available. Champagne is fermented in only four bottle sizes—the half-bottle, bottle, magnum and jeroboam. All larger sizes are refilled from bottles, and, consequently, in the sizes larger than the jeroboam, champagne does not always retain its sparkle and flavor quite so long. Similarly, this is true of 6½-ounce splits, which are also refilled from bottles. It is also important to remember that the larger the bottle in which champagne is fermented, the finer the quality.

OPENING AND SERVING CHAMPAGNE

 *T*he final step before serving champagne is opening the bottle. Here, too, there is an art: Since there is a great deal of pressure in the bottle, care must be taken that the cork does not fly out with a big pop and possibly injure someone. The champagne cork is tightly held in the neck of the bottle, making it particularly hard to remove without breaking the cork. To avoid these pitfalls, this is the accepted way to open and serve champagne:

1. Do not serve champagne too chilled, because its true taste and bouquet will be hidden.
2. Remove the wire cap and, with the bottle slightly tilted, hold the cork in your left hand and the bottom of the bottle in your right hand. Slowly turn the bottle (not the cork) and gradually ease out the cork, while pressing the cork into the bottle so that it will not pop out.
3. Before serving, smell the cork to determine if the wine is corky. When a cork is unsound, it smells earthy and gives the wine a musty odor and taste. This is known as a "corky" bottle.
4. Before serving, wipe the lip of the bottle clean. *Do not* wrap a napkin around the bottle—just wipe the bottle so that it does not drip and pour so that your guests can see the label. Wrapping the bottle can only mean that you are ashamed of the brand and want to hide the label.
5. Use the traditional long-stemmed tulip-shaped glass, because the bouquet can be better appreciated. Champagne should be poured slowly so that it won't foam up and lose its effervescence. The glass should be filled only halfway so that the wine can be swirled around to permit you to appreciate the bouquet.

The Wines
of Germany

The Rhenish frontier was the fifth division of Gaul, but the Roman legions were never successful in conquering any of the lands east of the Rhine. In fact, the whole Rhenish frontier was the most difficult to hold of all Gaul, and therefore the Roman influence here was never as strong.

During the Rhenish campaigns, the Romans established several important cities that are symbolic of the Roman influence. The most ancient city is Trier, which was fortified in 14 B.C. as the Roman city of Augusta Treverorum, so named after the Belgic tribe of Treveri. When Trier was made the capital of all Gaul in 293, the city was beautified with an imperial palace as well as many public buildings and became second only to Rome in grandeur.

The wines of the Rhine and Moselle are primarily indebted for their development to the strong and effective influence of the Church. While the spread of Christianity had started in the fourth and fifth centuries, its real growth came in the eighth century under the magnificent rule of Charlemagne, the first great emperor to champion Christianity. Some of the earliest vineyards planted by the Church date back to this time.

During his reign, Charlemagne made generous gifts of lands and vineyards to the Church, and his example was followed and continued by other princes and noblemen. This laid the foundation for the extraordinary wealth and power amassed by the Church, which reached its climax in the 18th century. For example, by the 13th century, the archbishop of Mainz owned the entire Rheingau, including Hochheim. The archbishops themselves became so wealthy that they could also afford to be generous, which resulted in the founding of some vineyards that are still famous today. In the 11th century, the Benedictine monks of St. Albans were given "the Bishop's Hill," which they renamed Johannisberg (Hill of St. John), and made it the site of the now-famous vineyard. Also in the 11th century, the forest of Steinberg was given to the Cistercian monks of Eberbach, which they cleared and walled in before planting the renowned Steinberg vineyard.

The climate and terrain of the Rhine and Moselle valleys are the most forbidding in all of Europe, but the monks had the knowledge, skill and tenacity not only to overcome these natural rigors, but also to turn them into advantages, developing some of the world's most delightfully aristocratic and distinctive white wines.

Later vineyard owners learned their skills from the monks, and the art of German viticulture continued to flourish and expand even further. At first, the new owners gave individual names to their finer vineyards, names by which their individual wines gained renown. By the middle of the 19th century, it was the accepted practice to label all quality wines with the name of the village, followed by the vineyard name. This led to the requirement that all such wines had to be registered, which became something like an unofficial classification. As the demand increased for these "registered" wines, other vineyard owners were encouraged to improve their vineyards so that they would qualify for registration.

The German Wine Law of 1909 stipulated the strict condition that sugar could be added to the grape only to supplement the natural sugar or to counteract excessive acidity. Only that quantity of sugar could be added that would produce the same sugar content the wine would have had if it had been made from similar grapes in a good vintage year.

THE NEW GERMAN WINE LAWS

*N*ew wine laws were promulgated in 1971 that have made some rather sweeping changes and that, at the same time, have more definitively regulated nomenclature. The specifics of the new laws are too lengthy to describe in detail, but basically they define three types of wine:

Deutscher Tafelwein—Ordinary table wine, of no prescribed strength, which cannot use a vineyard name.

Qualitätswein—Superior table wine, which must come from designated grapes and which must contain a minimum sugar content to permit the addition of more sugar.

Qualitätswein mit Prädikat—The top grade for exceptional wines, which must contain at least 10 percent alcohol, to which no sugar may be added, and which must come from certain grapes and from a designated district.

The 1971 laws also established four vineyard area designations:

1. *Gebiet*—A large wine-growing region.
2. *Bereich*—A smaller district within a Gebiet.

3. *Grosslage*—A smaller area formed by grouping together a number of neighboring vineyards, which then use the name of the best-known vineyard of the group.
4. *Einsellage*—An individual vineyard site.

The new 1971 laws represent quite an upheaval, particularly where the new vineyard area designations have effectively reduced the number of individual vineyards from the previously registered total of over 30,000 to a much smaller and more workable number.

These new laws represent an even further refinement of the typically precise definition of German labeling and the meticulous German vinification. Instead of just being a passport, the label on a bottle of German wine reads like a birth certificate—indicating where, when, why and by whom. This is the precise terminology that is indigenous to German wines:

Spätlese—Made from late-picked, fully ripened grapes.

Auslese—Made from a selected picking of fully ripened grapes.

Beerenauslese—Made from individually selected, overripe grapes.

Trockenbeerenauslese—Made from individually selected, semidried grapes that have been shriveled by the late autumn sun.

Edelbeerenauslese—Made from extraordinary individual overripe grapes that have not yet dried out.

Eiswein—Made from perfectly ripened grapes that have been partially frozen on the vine, resulting in a very elegant and rich wine.

Kabinett Wein—A separate bottling of specially selected wines from a particular estate.

Erzeuger Abfüllung—Bottled by the vineyard owner.

Kellerabfüllung—Cellar bottled by the shipper.

THE WINE REGIONS OF GERMANY

*T*he Riesling is the noble grape of Germany. It produces just about all the great wines, particularly in the vineyards of the Moselle and the Rheingau. The quality of its production is unsurpassed, but at the same time, the Riesling needs a great deal of sun and even then its yield is quite low. The Sylvaner is a much larger-producing, somewhat lesser-quality grape, which is used extensively in the Rheinhesse, Rheinpfalz and Franconia.

While the vintage in Germany starts later than in other white wine regions, the extent to which their special vinification procedures are used is dictated completely by the weather conditions during the growing season and at vintage time. When the weather conditions produce an ideal crop and the late fall is dry and warm, then the German vintners can use their special harvesting techniques to produce *Spätlese, Auslese, Beerenauslese, Trockenbeerenauslese* and, with a perfectly timed frost, the rather rare *Eiswein*. As an even further selective process, the casks from a particularly famous vineyard are not blended together as they are in Bordeaux and Burgundy; rather, individual casks are bottled out separately, with the price being determined by the quality of each cask.

There are three main wine-producing regions in Germany, each of which is further subdivided.

1. Rhine Valley includes the *Rheinpfalz,* the *Rheinhesse*, the *Nahe* and the *Rheingau.*
2. Moselle Valley includes the *Upper Moselle,* the *Saar* and the *Ruwer,* the *Middle Moselle* and the *Lower Moselle.*
3. Franconia includes the area around Würzburg on the Main River.

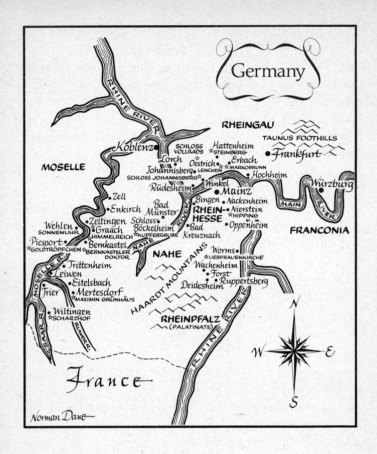

The map shows:

Germany

RHINE RIVER · Koblenz · MOSELLE · Zell · Enkirch · Wehlen · SONNENUHR · Zeltingen · Graach · HIMMELREICH · Piesport · GOLDTRÖPFCHEN · Bernkastel · BERNKASTELER DOKTOR · Trittenheim · Leiwen · Eitelsbach · Trier · Mertesdorf · MAXIMIN GRÜNHÄUS · Wiltingen · SCHARZHOF · SAAR · MOSELLE · RUWER

RHEINGAU · TAUNUS FOOTHILLS · Hattenheim · STEINBERG · Erbach · MARKOBRUNN · Frankfurt · Lorch · Oestrich · LENCHEN · Johannisberg · SCHLOSS VOLLRADS · SCHLOSS JOHANNISBERG · Hochheim · Rüdesheim · Winkel · Mainz · Bingen · Nackenheim · Bad Münster · Nierstein · HIPPING · Schloss · Oppenheim · Böckelheim · RHEIN-HESSE · KUPFERGRUBE · Bad Kreuznach · NAHE · FRANCONIA · Worms · UEBFRAUENKIRCHE · HAARDT MOUNTAINS · Wachenheim · Forst · Deidesheim · Ruppertsberg · RHEINPFALZ (PALATINATE) · RHINE RIVER · MAIN RIVER · Würzburg

France

Norman Dane

N · W · E · S

THE RHEINPFALZ

The Rheinpfalz, or Palatinate, is the largest vineyard area in Germany, but the majority of its production is *Tafelwein* (table wine), primarily using grapes other than Riesling. This is a very fertile area with a rather mild climate, because the Haardt Mountains protect it from the winds from the north and the rain and snow from the west. The changing soil composition divides the Rheinpfalz into three distinct areas: the Oberhaardt, the Mittelhaardt and the Unterhaardt, with all of the finest vineyards being in the Mittelhaardt, where the Riesling grape is used extensively.

This is also a land of vast estate owners, where the estates of Bürklin-Wolf, von Basserman-Jordan and von Buhl comprise the largest part of the best vineyards in the Mittelhaardt. No particular vineyards have gained a prominence equal to those in the Rheingau or in the Rheinhesse, but the wines produced in the villages of Ruppertsberg, Deidesheim, Forst and Wachenheim are considered the best of the Rheinpfalz.

THE RHEINHESSE

The Rheinhesse lies in the bend of the Rhine, on the left bank, hemmed in by the wine regions of the Rheinpfalz and the Nahe. The Rheinhesse is the second largest-producing area of the Rhine, but since many of its vineyards are planted with Sylvaner, in general the quality does not compare with that of the Rheingau. This does not hold true for the important villages of Oppenheim, Nierstein and Nackenheim, all of which produce soft, rich wines that have always been popular in the United States.

The best-known vineyards lie at the southern end of Rheinhesse around the town of Worms. The famous Liebfrauenkirche (Church of Our Lovely Lady) stands within the city limits and is surrounded by three vineyards whose wines have been renowned for centuries. The real importance of these vineyards lies in their having given rise to the name Liebfraumilch, which is certainly the best-known name in German wine.

The name Liebfraumilch has been in use for over 200 years and originally applied only to a blend of wines from Rheinhesse. The German Wine Law of 1909 extended the terminology and established that the name Liebfraumilch could be applied to all Rhine wines of good quality and delightful character. This more encompassing definition provides a great deal of latitude in the quality determination of Liebfraumilch, and since it is always a blended wine, the reliability of quality can come only from the reliability of the shipper.

The origin of the name Liebfraumilch is still rather controversial. The most obvious and accepted theory is the translation, "Milk of Our Lovely Lady." The other theory maintains that *milch* is derived from *minch,* which meant "monk" in the local dialect. With this meaning, the derivation of Liebfraumilch is from *Liebfrauenminch,* which would then refer to wine made by the monks from the vineyards surrounding the Liebfrauenkirche. Be that as it may, Liebfraumilch remains the most popular of all German wines.

THE NAHE

The Nahe district, having many scattered vineyard areas along both banks of the Nahe River until it flows into the Rhine at Bingen, is quite different from the other vineyard areas in the Rhine Valley. The most illustrious vineyard is Kupfergrube, which is planted on the site of some old copper diggings in the village of Schlossböckelheim. Two other fine vineyards are Hermannshöhle and Herrmannsberg in Niederhausen. There are also other good vineyards in the village of Norheim.

At Bad Münster the Nahe is forced by the staggeringly high red cliff, the Rotenfels, to take an abrupt ninety-degree turn. Here, at the base of the cliff, is planted the small but famous vineyard of Rotenfelser Bastei. Farther up the Nahe is the village of Bad Kreuznach, which is the center of the Nahe wine trade and where, besides its many vineyards, most of the leading growers have their cellars.

THE RHEINGAU

The Rheingau is the lofty climax of the vineyards on the Rhine. Because of the Taunus Mountains, the Rhine turns east for some thirty miles until it reaches the Rüdesheimer Berg, where it turns back north. In the Rheingau, the vineyards are planted on the north bank of the Rhine, where they are protected from the cold north winds by the Taunus foothills and where they enjoy the full southern exposure. With this perfect situation, the Rheingau is Germany's most magnificent vineyard area, and the wines of the Rheingau are considered the noblest in Germany.

The many important vineyard villages of the Rheingau start at Hochheim, which is actually on the Main River, just before it flows into the Rhine. In 1273, the Cologne cathedral sold Hochheim and its vineyards to the Mainz cathedral, and the names of the two finest vineyards still show their ecclesiastical origin: Domdechaney ("cathedral deanery") and Kirchenstück ("church piece"). The famous estate known as the "Queen Victoria Vineyard" (*Königin-Viktoria-Berg*) is also located in Hochheim and is so named because the vineyard was christened in 1850 by Queen Victoria.

Farther down the Rhine comes Erbach. Its famous vineyard is Markobrunn, which is a narrow strip of vines lying alongside the bank of the river right up to the neighboring village of Hattenheim—hence the name Markobrunn, which means "boundary fountain." Back up in the hills of Hattenheim stands the most illustrious of all the vineyards of the German state—the famous Steinberger vineyard, which is walled in by a Cistercian wall like Clos de Vougeot. In a wooded hollow below the vineyard stands the old monastery of Kloster Eberbach, which traces its history back over 600 years and symbolizes the great tradition of German wines. The finest wines of Steinberger are labeled *Kabinett,* with additional designations of *Spätlese, Auslese,* etc., and almost all Steinberger wines are bottled out from separate casks and so labeled with the cask number.

After the village of Oestrich, whose most famous vineyard is Lenchen, comes the important village of Winkel, whose greatest vineyard is the famous Schloss Vollrads. This magnificent estate totals eighty-one acres of vines and is the largest privately owned vineyard of the Rheingau. The estate-bottled wines of Schloss Vollrads are sold under five different colored capsules to indicate their individual grade of excellence.

Standing back off the Rhine, in the neighboring village of Johannisberg, is the spectacular vineyard of Schloss Johannisberg, a beautifully symmetrical vineyard covering the entire hillside with the medieval *Schloss* (castle) standing at the crest. In the 11th century, the archbishop of Mainz gave this "Bishop's Hill" to the Benedictine monks of St. Albans, who renamed it Johannisberg (Hill of St. John) and planted the first vineyards. After it passed through many hands, the emperor of Austria presented it in 1815 to Fürst von Metternich, whose descendants still own it today. The three *cuvées* of Schloss Johannisberg are identified by three different colored seals—red, green and pink, and some of the finest wines are further selected to be bottled as *Kabinett* wines.

The westernmost important town in the Rheingau is Rüdesheim, where most of the finest vineyards are terraced right into the face of the steep hillside, called the Berg. For this reason, these wines are distinguished from those of the rest of the parish by being designated Rüdesheimer Berg.

THE UPPER MOSELLE

The Moselle Valley, which is divided into four sections, is the most forbidding terrain of all the German wine areas, because the soil is less rich, the vineyard slopes are steeper and rockier and the climate is generally colder. Therefore, the vines must be cultivated far more carefully to protect them from the wind and to expose them to the maximum amount of sun. All Moselle wines have a delightful dryness and fragrance, and they are the lightest of all German wines, only rarely exceeding 10 percent alcohol. It is convenient to know that Moselle wines are always shipped in dark green bottles, whereas Rhine wines are shipped in brown bottles.

The Upper Moselle stretches from the Luxembourg

border to the town of Leiwen. This section generally produces only lesser wines that are mainly used for *Sekt* (champagne).

THE SAAR AND THE RUWER

The separate areas of the Saar River and the Ruwer River both produce some very distinguished wines. These two valleys both wage a hard battle against the elements, because these are the coldest vineyard areas in Germany. Consequently, most vintages are unsuccessful and the wine is usually sold to the *Sekt* producers. But once every three or four years, the weather is perfect and truly superlative wines are produced.

In the Saar region, the finest vineyards are in the village of Wiltingen. Egon Müller owns the famous estate of Scharzhof, which is closely rivaled by the equally renowned estate of Braune Kupp. Although the Ruwer is an even smaller region, it boasts a few more celebrated vineyards. In Mertesdorf is the great estate of Maximin Grünhäus, where the larger part of the hill is called Herrenberg and the top part is called Abtsberg. In the neighboring town of Eitelsbach is the equally renowned estate of Karthäuserhofberg, and in the town of Trier itself is the well-known Tiergarten vineyard.

All the finest Moselles come from the vineyards of the Middle Moselle, which stretches from Leiwen to Enkirch. Here the spectacular hillsides of slate, which sometimes rise 700 feet above the river, provide the perfect conditions for the Riesling vine and for producing the great Moselles.

The first village of importance is Piesport, which derived its name from Pepin, the first king of the Carolingian dynasty in 752. The world-famed Goldtröpfchen ("little gold drop") vineyard was once only the central part of the vineyard just above the village, but now virtually all of this magnificent vineyard is entitled to the name Goldtröpfchen.

Bernkastel is the chief city of the Middle Moselle, and its most famous vineyard is the world-renowned Bernkasteler Doktor, which is considered the finest vineyard in all of Germany. The name is traced back by legend to 1360, when the archbishop of Trier fell ill with a fever while visiting Bernkastel and the doctors were unable to cure him. His old friend Ritter von Hunolstein heard of the archbishop's illness and brought him a bottle of his finest Bernkastel wine, telling him the wine would cure him. The archbishop fell into a sound sleep, and when he awoke, his fever had gone and he exclaimed, "This wine, this splendid doctor cured me!" This legend explains why this famous vineyard became known as the Bernkasteler Doktor vineyard. It is merely coincidence that part of the vineyard was owned many years later by Dr. Thanisch.

The Bernkasteler Doktor vineyard was the property of the Grafs von der Leyen until 1794, when it was declared "public property" under the edict of Napoleon. From 1794 until 1880 the Doktor vineyard was leased out to a number of individuals and finally the entire vineyard was sold to Dr. Hugo Thanisch in 1882. In 1899, Deinhard & Company acquired 55 percent of the famous vineyard at a price of 100 gold marks per vine, which was then the highest price that had ever been paid for any vineyard. With their purchase, Deinhard also obtained large, valuable stocks of older vintages along with the original Bernkasteler Doktor cellars, located in the hillside beneath this famous vineyard.

The vineyards in Bernkastel cover the steep 700-foot-high hillsides above the town and stretch out for about two miles on either side. The view from the town below is probably one of the most picturesquely beautiful of all vineyard areas. The wines of Bernkastel are the most popular and best known of all Moselle wines and are the most typical of the delightful dryness and fragrance for which Moselles are so famed.

After Bernkastel, the Moselle changes course, so that the famous vineyards in the villages of Graach and Wehlen are on the northern bank of the river. At Graach the most famous vineyard is Himmelreich, and at Wehlen the most famous vineyard is Sonnenuhr, which takes its name from the sun dial set in the heart of the steep sunny hillside. These two vineyards are certainly equal to the finest of the Moselle. Zeltingen is the last important town, which has a wonderful expanse of vineyards, probably the largest of the Moselle. Although they produce a large quantity of wine, there are no particularly outstanding vineyards.

THE LOWER MOSELLE

The village of Zell just borders on the Middle Moselle and its importance is due to the popular wine Zeller Schwarze Katz. This curious name came about when a wine buyer was sampling wines from various *Fuders* (casks) at Zell, trying to decide which one to buy. Not having any other identification, he pointed to a *Fuder* on which a black cat was sitting—and hence the name Zeller Schwarze Katz, which means "the black cat of Zell."

In general, there are no outstanding vineyards in the Lower Moselle, but the area is particularly identified with the popular wine, Moselblümchen, which means "little flower of the Moselle." This name does not refer to a vineyard, but similar to Liebfraumilch, it is a generic name for a blend of various Moselle wines, shipped by most firms.

FRANCONIA

Franconia was an independent duchy in the 10th century, and in spite of its political turmoils, its fine vineyards have continued to flourish on the banks of the Main River, particularly around Würzburg.

Geographically, Franconia is quite separate from the great vineyard areas of the Rhine and Moselle. But it is also separated by tradition, since it makes the only great wine from Sylvaner and it is also the only German wine not to use the traditional flute bottle.

Franconian wines use their own flat-sided *Bocksbeutel*. It is generally thought that the shape and name originated from the old German *Bockesbeutel,* which was a bag used to carry prayer books and other volumes. The name Steinwein is now generally used for all Franconian wines, having originated from the famous Stein vineyard in Würzburg. Today all the finest Steinwein comes from the Steinmantel, which includes the ten or twelve villages along the bends of the Main River above and below Würzburg.

The Wines of Spain

The vine grows abundantly throughout Spain because the climate, which varies from almost tropical to temperate, is ideal and because the soil is rather poor. Spain is probably the oldest wine-producing country in Western Europe, and the history of its wine-making can be traced as far back as prehistoric times. Spain constitutes most of the Iberian Peninsula, which was named for the Iberians, the first important inhabitants; apparently the Phoenicians were the first settlers, having come here in the 11th century B.C. One of the Phoenician's earliest cities was Gades (now Cadiz), which is considered the oldest surviving town in Europe, with a continuity of life and name from its very beginnings.

The Greeks founded the first true colonies in Spain, but their civilization was broken by the Carthaginians during the fourth century B.C. Then the Romans came and drove out the Carthaginians during the second Punic War, in the second century B.C. This started the latinization of Spain, which lasted despite the fall of the Roman Empire in the fourth century A.D., when the barbarians invaded and devastated Spain, as they did most of the rest of Europe. Finally, in the eighth century, Spain was conquered and unified by the Moors,

whose strong dominion lasted until the Christian re-
conquest in the twelfth century, which marked the
beginning of modern Spain.

More than any other country in Europe, Spain
has been exposed to a tumultuous history and to many
cultures, each of which has left its mark. Because the
climate and soil were so favorable, the vine lasted
through all these upheavals and was continuously cultivated, even during the Moorish reign. The Phoenicians, who knew a great deal about wines, must have
been the first to exert their wine-making influence.
They were followed by the Greeks and then by the
Romans, who were the greatest *vignerons* of the Old
World.

In Roman days, starting in the first century B.C.,
wine was a major Spanish export and probably made up
a good part of the tribute Spain was forced to pay to
Rome. By the second century A.D., during the heyday
of the Roman Empire, it is estimated that twenty million amphoras of Spanish wine had been shipped to
Rome. Wine production continued to flourish after the
fall of the Roman Empire and, curiously enough, even
after the Moorish conquest in the eighth century, since
it appears that the Moslem rule of abstinence was hon-
ored more in the breach than in the observance. When
the Moors were driven out, the people again enjoyed
their wine in peace, and the cultivation of the grape
both increased and improved.

During the 15th and 16th centuries, Spain was the
strongest country in Europe, and this strength fostered
the growth of wine production and trade. At this time,
Spanish wine was exported to France and England;
then, with the discovery of the New World, it was exported extensively to Mexico and Central America. In
1875, history played another interesting role in the
development of Spain's wine trade, when the phylloxera
devastated the vineyards of Europe but did not spread
down into Spain. As a result, the rest of Europe drew

on the vineyards of Spain for its wines, and Spain entered its second great era of wine growth.

Even though vines are cultivated in Spain on more land area than in any other country, including Italy, Spain's wine production is only one-third that of Italy. This is because it is the custom in Spain to plant the vines haphazardly mixed in with other crops. Except for the highly organized wine regions of Jerez and the Rioja, the wine regions of Spain are rather loosely defined, and their production methods are somewhat crude. Starting at the very southern tip of the Iberian Peninsula, we will now briefly describe the more important wine regions of Spain.

JEREZ

Located in the province of Andalucía, at the very southern tip of Spain, Jerez de la Frontera is the heart of the sherry trade. *Vino de Jerez*, the oldest wine in Spain, is certainly the crown jewel of all Spanish wines.

The name sherry is actually the anglicized form of Jerez. Since sherry is a fortified wine and not a table wine, a full and complete description is not included in this book.

MALAGA

Malaga is one of those special wines with a great history but with little importance in the present. The wines of Malaga are rather sweet and heavy, but unfortunately they are no longer popular. In the second century A.D., they were very much in demand in Imperial Rome; in later years, Malaga had a great trade with England, where these rich fruity wines were very much in favor. However, today, with the trend toward less sweet wines, they have almost faded into obscurity.

MONTILLA

Montilla is at the peak of a triangle about one hundred miles north of both Jerez and Malaga, and its wines are often called the "poor man's sherries." They are also known as the "sherries of Cordoba," since Cordoba is the commercial center of this wine-growing district. Once again, because these are fortified wines, we will not describe them in detail, except to point out that they are made much like sherry and fall into similar categories of taste and quality.

LA MANCHA

The large wine-growing district of La Mancha is to Spain what the Midi wine district is to France. As such, La Mancha supplies Spain with large quantities of sound, inexpensive wine, mostly sold straight from the barrel in wine shops throughout Spain. The name La Mancha comes from the Moorish word *marzo,* which means "dry land"; the La Mancha district is a large, arid plain ideally suited to large-volume production of lesser quality wines. During the phylloxera scourge, these wines in particular were exported to France to replace the depleted stocks of the French *vin de table.* Although most of the wine is rather pedestrian, some creditable wine is produced around the town of Valdepeñas. There is still a large wine trade in *pelligos,* which are curious wine containers made from the whole skin of a pig. La Mancha is also famous in story as the world of Don Quixote.

149

TARRAGONA

Two quite different types of wine are made in the rather large district of Tarragona, which is in north-eastern Spain, on the Mediterranean coast. One is the classic Tarragona, which is a rather sweet and heavy wine; the other type is comprised of a number of rather pedestrian red and white table wines. The classic Tarragona once had a very large trade in England, where it became known as the "poor man's port," because by mistake it carried a lower excise tax that made it less expensive. When the correct tax was finally levied and Tarragona was put in a higher price category, sales fell off sharply, because Tarragona could not overcome its "poor" image. The other wines of Tarragona have also suffered from this stigma, with the result that Tarragona has practically no export market and virtually the entire production is consumed locally in Spain.

RIOJA

The Rioja has always been considered the finest-quality wine region in all of Spain. It lies just south of the French border, surrounded in the north by the mountains of Sierra Cantabria, which protect the Rioja Valley below from the harsh winter winds. The Rioja has a mountainous atmosphere; the finest vineyards are located in the upper valley, about 1,500 feet above sea level. The perfection of the Rioja is that it has an ample rainfall along with long spring and autumn seasons, which is quite different from the endless dry summers in the other vineyard areas to the south. The entire vineyard area of the Rioja stretches eastward for eighty miles, from the chief wine center of Haro to the eastern-most city of Alfaro.

The vineyards are planted on both sides of the Rio Ebro, which flows from one end of the region to the other and which is joined at its westernmost point by the small Rio Oja, from whose shortened name comes the name Rioja. The vines are grown and wine is made throughout this beautiful land of gentle hills, many of which are capped with castles and churches, making it one of the most picturesque wine-growing areas in the world.

By virtue of terrain, soil and altitude, the Rioja district is divided into three parts. Rioja Alta lies in the western portion, farthest upriver, where the terrain is higher and the rainfall ideal. It is centered around the wine town of Haro; here are produced the lightest and best wines of the Rioja.

On the other side of the Rio Ebro and just to the north is Rioja Alavesa, whose wines are slightly bolder but still have a certain smoothness.

The third area is Rioja Baja, whose *bodegas*—or shipping houses—are centered around the large town of Logroño. Here the climate is more Mediterranean, warmer and with less rainfall. As a result, the wines of Rioja Baja are harsher and stronger, without the breeding and finesse of the wines of Rioja Alta.

Wines have been made in the Rioja for centuries. They had the distinction of being much sought after by the kings and grandees of Spain. In 1102 when King Sancho of Navarre founded a monastery in the Rioja, its fine vineyards were mentioned in the deeds. By the 16th and 17th centuries, Rioja wines had achieved great recognition and were already world-famous. It is particularly interesting to note that in 1560 the Riojans adopted one of the earliest of all trademarks, marking their casks with their own Denomination of Origin. With this trademark, the Riojans founded the first wine trade association in Spain and one of the earliest in all Europe.

Also during these early days, in order to protect the authenticity of their finest wines, a few of the leading shippers encased the bottles of their finer wines in a wire mesh, which was sealed at the bottom with the private seal of the *bodega*. Although the seals have been abandoned, the wire mesh is still used to embellish some of the old *reservas*, the finest of all Riojas. The early trademark and the wire mesh are living examples of the 400-year-old traditions of the Rioja.

The wines of the Rioja owe a great deal of their excellence to the Bordeaux *vignerons*, who left their vineyards when they were devastated by the phylloxera and journeyed across the Pyrenees to continue their wine-making in the Rioja. Although they found a different terrain, a somewhat different climate and different wine stocks, to all of these they lent their Bordeaux expertise, helping the Riojans to produce even finer wines in the true Bordeaux tradition.

The *vignerons* from Bordeaux left a great mark on Rioja wines but did not transplant their system of château bottling. Since there are no specific wine estates in the Rioja, the wine trade operates through a limited number of large *bodegas* (shippers), which buy most of their grapes from farmers, supplementing what they grow themselves, and then blend the wine to their own house style. Since the art of Rioja wine is in the blending by the shipper, rather than in the cultivation of a specific grape, the shipper's name and his reputation are of critical importance. While vineyard names refer to any particular vineyard, but are used by the *bodegas* as brand names for their better wines.

The best Rioja wines are the red wines, which are made from a mixture of grape varieties, the most familiar of which is the Garnacha, similar to the Grenache of the Rhone. The red Riojas are still made pretty much as red wines were made in Bordeaux a hundred years ago. They are aged for several years in the barrel until their fruitiness and darkness develop into a softer wine with a lighter, tawny color. Because the soil is rather fertile and the weather quite consistent, vintages do not vary very much from year to year. The importance of vintage years in Rioja wines is mainly to indicate the age of the wine, rather than a difference between various vintage years. Another difference in Riojan viticulture is that the addition of sugar to the fermenting wine is not permitted, as it is in regions of France and Germany. However, in Spain, as in Chianti, a certain amount of *mistela,* or unfermented must, is blended with the new wine to continue fermentation, in order to achieve the proper alcoholic strength. In addition, a certain proportion of old *reserva* wines are often blended with younger Rioja wines to add more body and flavor.

Pronouncing Glossary

The following glossary of wine names and related vocabulary has been prepared with a brief description of each term, together with the phonetic spelling to facilitate correct pronunciation.

All wine terms and wine names mentioned in the book appear alphabetically. However, please note that in the case of châteaux, these appear alphabetically by the name of the château, and each château is indicated with an asterisk (*). Also, when *le, la* or *les* is part of the name, the article follows in parentheses.

To help pronounce these words correctly, use the phonetic rendition in parentheses. Pronounce the separated syllables as if they were written in English and emphasize the italicized syllables. For example: in English, Paris is pronounced *Pa*-ris, but in French, Paris is pronounced Pa-*ree*—stressing the final syllable as is usual in French pronunciation. There are also several other useful points:

1. Whenever you see a *ü* in the phonetics, pronounce it like *ee* with your lips in a tight circle. With a little practice, this will give you an approximation of the French "u" and the "ü" in German.
2. When you see "ng" at the end of a syllable in the French phonetics, pronounce the "n" through your nose, as in *song* or *long* in English.

3. The French "j" is pronounced like "s," as in *treasure* or *measure*. This is indicated in the phonetics as "zh."
4. When you see a "kh" in the German phonetics, pronounce it with a guttural sound.

agrafe (ah-*grahf*) Metal cork clip used for secondary champagne fermentation

Alby (Al-*bee*) Leading producer and shipper (Languedoc)

Alfaro (Ahl-*fah*-ro) Easternmost city in Rio Baja

Aloxe-Corton (Ah-lohx-Cor-*tohng*) Red wine commune in the Côte de Beaune.

Alsace (Ahl-*zahss*) Vineyard region in northeastern France

Amphora (Am-*fo*-ra) Large earthenware wine jug

Anjou (Ahn-*zhoo*) Vineyard area in the Loire Valley

Anjou-Saumur (Ahn-*zhoo*-So-*mür*) Vineyard region of the Loire Valley

Antinori (Ahn-tee-*no*-ree) Leading producer and shipper (Chianti)

Apellation Contrôlée (Ah-pel-ah-*s'yohng* Kohn-tro-*lay*) Legal designation of French vineyard areas

Asti Spumante (*Ah*-stee Spoo-*mahn*-tee) A sparkling white wine from Piedmont

Auslese (*Owss*-lay-zeh) Selected picking of fully ripened grapes

*Ausone (Oh-*zone*) A First Classified Great Growth in St. Emilion

Auxey-Duresses (Ohk-*zay*-Dü-ress) Small red wine commune in Côte de Beaune

Avignon (Ah-veen-*yong*) Major city of Côtes du Rhône

Bacchus (*Ba*-kus) The Roman god of wine

Ban de Vendange (Bahng duh Vahng-*dahnzh*) The prescribed day on which to start the vintage

Bandol (Bahn-*dohl*) A red wine appellation in Côtes de Provence

Barbaresco (Bar-ba-*ress*-ko) A fine red wine from Piedmont

Barbera (Bar-*beh*-ra) A red wine grape and red wine from Piedmont

Bardolino (Bar-doh-*lee*-no) A Veronese red wine

Barolo (Ba-*ro*-lo) A fine red wine from Piedmont

barrique (ba-*reek*) Bordeaux wine barrel holding fifty-four gallons

Bâtard-Montrachet (Ba-*tar*-Mohng-tra-*shay*) White *Grand Cru* in Puligny-Montrachet

Beaujolais (Bo-zho-*lay*) Major red wine region of southern Burgundy

Beaune (Bone) The capital of Burgundy

Beerenauslese (Beh-ren-*owss*-lay-zeh) Individually selected overripe grapes

Bellet (Bell-*lay*) Small appellation in Côtes de Provence

Bereich (Beh-*rye'kh*) A smaller district within a *Gebiet* (Germany)

Bernkastel (*Behrn*-kas-tel) The chief vineyard city of the Middle Moselle

Bernkasteler Doktor (*Behrn*-kast-ler Dok-*tor*) World-famous Moselle vineyard in Bernkastel

*Beychevelle (Baysh-*vel*) A Classified Fourth Growth in Médoc (St. Julien)

Bianco Toscano (*B'yahng*-ko Tohs-*ka*-no) A dry white wine from Tuscany

Bienvenues (Les) (B'yeng-veh-*nü*) White *Grand Cru* in Puligny-Montrachet

Blanc (Blahng) White

Blanc Fumé (Blahng Fü-*may*) The Sauvignon Blanc as it is known in the Loire Valley

Blanchot (Blawng-*sho*) *Grand Cru* in Chablis

Bocksbeutel (*Box*-boy-tel) The flat-sided squat bottle used in Franconia

Bodegas (Bo-*day*-gahs) Large wine cellars of one shipper

Bolgheri (Bohl-*geh*-ree) Antinori estate in Tuscany

Bollinger (Bo-lahng-*zhay*) The leading quality French champagne

Bonnes-Mares (Les) (Bun Mar) Red *Grand Cru* in Chambolle-Musigny

Bordeaux (Bor-*doh*) Major city in the department of Gironde

Bourgogne Aligoté (Boor-*goy'n* Ah-lee-go-*tay*) A lesser wine from the Chablis region

Bourgogne-Blanc (Boor-*goy'n* Blahng) White Burgundy from the Côte Chalonnaise

Bougros (Boo-*gro*) *Grand Cru* in Chablis

Bourgueil (Boor-*goy*) Red wine commune in Coteaux de Touraine

*Brane-Cantenac (Brahn-Kahn-tuh-*nahk*) A Classified Second Growth in Médoc (Margaux)

Braune Kupp (*Brow*-neh Koop) An important vineyard in Wiltingen (Saar)

Brochon (Bro-*shohng*) Small commune in the Côte de Nuits

Brouilly (Broo-*yee*) The largest commune in Beaujolais

Brut (Brüt) The driest champagne

Cabernet Franc (Ka-*bair*-nay Frahng) A red wine grape of Bordeaux

Cabernet Sauvignon (Ka-*bair*-nay So-veen-*yohng*) The most important red wine grape of Bordeaux

Cádiz (*Ka*-deez) Oldest town in Europe (Spain)

*Calon-Ségur (Ka-lohng Say-*gür*) A Classified Third Growth in Médoc (St. Estèphe)

Campania (Kahm-*pahn*-ya) A department in southern Italy

*Canon (Ka-*nohng*) A Classified First Great Growth in St. Emilion

*Carbonnieux (Kar-bohn-*yuh*) A Classified Growth in Graves (white)

Cassis (Ka-*sees*) White wine appellation in Côtes de Provence

Castello Della Sala (Ka-*stel*-lo *day*-la Sa-la) Antinori estate in Orvieto

*Certan-de-May (Sair-*tahng* duh May) A First Growth in Pomerol

Chablis (Sha-*blee*) White wine region north of the Côte d'Or

Chaintré (Shant-*tray*) White wine commune in the Côte Mâconnaise

Chambertin (Shahm-bair-*teng*) Red *Grand Cru* in Gevrey-Chambertin

Chambolle-Musigny (Shahm-*bohl* Mü-seen-*yee*) Red wine commune in the Côte de Nuits

Champagne (Shahm-*pahn*-yuh) The vineyard region northeast of Paris

Chanson (Shawn-*sohng*) Leading producer - and shipper (Burgundy)

Charmes (Sharm) White *Premier Cru* in Meursault

Charmes-Chambertin (Sharm-Shahm-bair-*teng*) Red *Grand Cru* in Gevrey-Chambertin

Chassagne-Montrachet (Sha-sign-Mohng-tra-*shay*) White wine commune in the Côte de Beaune.

*Chasse-Spleen (Shass-*Spleen*) A Classified *Cru Exceptionnel* in Médoc

Chasselas (Shahss-*la*) White grape grown in Pouilly-sur-Loire

château (sha-*toh*) A specified viticultural holding

Châteauneuf-du-Pape (Sha-toh-*nuhf* dü Pahp) Red wine area in the Côtes du Rhône

Chénas (Shay-*na*) A commune in Beaujolais

*Cheval Blanc (Shuh-*vahl* Blahng) A Classified First Great Growth in St. Emilion

Chevalier-Montrachet (Shuh-vahl-*yay* Mohng-tra-*shay*) White *Grand Cru* in Puligny-Montrachet

Chevaliers de Méduse (Shuh-vahl-*yay* duh May-*düz*) Oldest French Bacchanalian Order (Provence)

Chevaliers du Tastevin (Shuh-vahl-*yay* dü Tahst-*veng*) Order of Burgundian Wine Lovers

Chianti (*K'yahn*-tee) The famous red wine from Tuscany

Chinon (Shee-*nohng*) Red wine commune in Coteaux de Touraine

Chiroubles (Shee-*roobl*) A commune in Beaujolais

Classico Chianti (*Kla*-see-ko *K'yahn*-tee) The Superior Chianti from the Classico district

climat (klee-*ma*) A small vineyard holding in Burgundy

*Climens (Klee-*mahng*) A classi-fied First Growth in Sauternes

Clos (Les) (Klo) A *Grand Cru* in Chablis

Clos de Bèze (Klo duh Behz) Red *Grand Cru* in Gevrey-Chambertin

Clos de la Roche (Klo duh la Rohsh) Red *Grand Cru* in Morey-St. Denis

Clos des Mouches (Klo day Moosh) Red *Premier Cru* in Beaune

Clos de Tart (Klo duh Tar) Red *Grand Cru* in Morey-St. Denis

Clos de Vougeot (Klo duh Voo-*zho*) Red *Grand Cru* in Vougeot

Clos du Roi (Le) (Klo dü Rwa) Red *Premier Cru* in Aloxe-Corton

Clos Gaensbroennel (Klo Gahng-bro-*nel*) *Grand Cru* Gewürztraminer in Alsace

Clos St. Denis (Klo Sahng Du-*nee*) Red *Grand Cru* in Morey-St. Denis

Clos Sainte-Odile (Klo Sahnt O-*deel*) *Grand Cru* Gewürztraminer in Alsace

commune (ko-*müne*) A delimited vineyard area in the Côte d'Or

Condrieu (Kohn-dree-*yuh*) White wine vineyard area in Côtes du Rhône

Córdoba (*Kor*-doh-ba) Chief town of Montilla

Corton (Le) (Kor-*tohng*) Red *Grand Cru* in Aloxe-Corton

Corton-Charlemagne (Kor-*tohng*-Shar-luh-*mahn*-yuh) White *Grand Cru* from Aloxe-Corton

Corvo (*Kor*-vo) A fine "château-bottled" red wine (Sicily)

*Cos d'Estournel (Kos-Dess-toor-*nel*) A Classified Second Growth in Médoc (St. Estèphe)

*Cos-Labory (Kos-La-bo-*ree*) A Classified Fifth Growth in Médoc (St. Estèphe)

Côte Chalonnaise (Koht Sha-lohn-*nay*) Northwestern region of southern Burgundy

Côte de Beaune (Koht duh *Bone*) The southern region of the Côte d'Or

Côte de Beaune-Villages (Koht duh *Bone*-Vee-*lahzh*) Appellation for Côte de Beaune (red)

Côte de Brouilly (Koht duh Broo-*yee*) A superior commune in Beaujolais

Côte Mâconnaise (Koht Ma-ko-*nay*) North central region of southern Burgundy

Côte de Nuits (Koht duh N'wee) Northern region of the Côte d'Or

Côte de Nuits-Villages (Koht duh N'wee-Vee-*lahzh*) Appellation for Côte de Nuits (red)

Côtes de Provence (Koht duh Pro-*vahngss*) The wine region of Provence

Côte d'Or (Koht dor) The heart of the Burgundy region

Côte Rôtie (Koht ro-*tee*) Red wine vineyard area in the Côtes du Rhône

Coteaux de Touraine (Ko-*toh* duh Too-*rain*) A vineyard area of the Loire

Côtes du Rhône (Koht dü Rohn) Vineyard region in the Rhone Valley

*****Coutet** (Koo-*tay*) A Classified First Growth in Sauternes

Criots (Les) (Cree-*yo*) White *Grand Cru* in Puligny-Montrachet

cuvée (kü-*vay*) The first pressing in Champagne

Demi-Sec (*Duh*-mee-*Sek*) Designation for the sweetest champagne

Dordogne (Dor-*doyn*) A tributary of the Gironde River

dégorgement (day-gorzh-*mahng*)

Removing champagne cork with frozen sediment

Deinhard (*Dine*-hardt) Leading producer and shipper (Rhine and Moselle)

deuxième taille (*duhz*-yem *tie*) The third pressing in Champagne

Dionysus (Dye-yo-*nye*-zus) The Greek god of wine

Dominode (La) (Doh-mee-*nohd*) A red *Premier Cru* in Savigny

Dom Pérignon (Dohm Pay-reen-*yohng*) The Benedictine monk famous in Champagne

dosage de tirage (doh-*zahzh* duh tee-*rahzh*) Dosage for uniform secondary fermentation

*****Ducru-Beaucaillou** (Dü-krü-Bo-kye-*yoo*) A Classified Second Growth in Médoc (St. Julien)

*****Durfort-Vivens** (Dür-*for*-Vee-*vahng*) A Classified Second Growth in Médoc (Margaux)

Echézeaux (Les) (Ay-sheh-*zo*) Red *Grand Cru* in Flagey-Echézeaux

Edelbeerenauslese (Ay-del-*behr*-en-*owss*-lay-zeh) Extraordinary individual overripe grapes

Einsellage (*Ine*-zel-la-guh) An individual vineyard site in Germany

Eiswein (*Ice*-vine) Perfectly ripened, partially frozen grapes

Emilia-Romagna (Ay-*meel*-ya Ro-*mahn*-ya) A department in north central Italy

Enkirch (*En*-keerkh) A vineyard village of the Middle Moselle

en primeur (ahng pree-*muhr*) The first sale of a château-bottled Bordeaux

Entre-deux-Mers (*Ahn*-truh duh *Mair*) Lesser red wine district of Bordeaux

Epenots (Les) (Eh-puh-*no*) Red *Premier Cru* in Pommard

épluchage (ay-plü-*shahzh*) Selecting the perfect grapes in Champagne

Erbach (*Air*-bahkh) A vineyard village of the Rheingau

Erzeuger Abfüllung (Air-*tsoi*-ger Ahb-*fül*-loonk) Bottled by the vineyard owner

Est! Est!! Est!!! (Est Est Est) A delightful white wine from Montefiascone

Falerno (Fa-*lair*-no) An ancient red wine from Campania

°**Falfas** (Fahl-*fa*) A Classified Growth in the Côtes de Bourg

Fèves (Les) (Fev) Red *Premier Cru* in Beaune

°**Figeac** (Fee-*zhahk*) A First Classified Great Growth in St. Emilion

Fixin (Feek-*zeng*) The northernmost commune in the Côte de Nuits

Flagey-Echézeaux (Fla-zhey-Ay-sheh-*zo*) A small red wine commune in the Côte de Nuits

Fleurie (Fluh-*ree*) A commune in Beaujolais

°**Fleur-Pourret (La)** (Flerr poo-*ray*) A Classified Principal Growth in St. Emilion

Frascati (Fra-*ska*-tee) A strong red wine from Latium

Frecciarossa (Fray-cha-*ro*-sa) "Château-bottled" red and white wine (Lombardy)

Fuder (*Foo*-der) A large wooden cask used in the Moselle

Fuissé (Fwee-*say*) White wine village in the Côte Mâconnais

Gamay (Ga-*may*) A red wine grape used mainly in Beaujolais

Garnacha (Gar-*na*-chah) Red wine grape in Rioja

Garonne (Ga-*rawn*) A tributary of the Gironde River

°**Gazin** (Ga-*zeng*) A First Growth in Pomerol

Gebiet (Geh-*beet*) A wine-growing region in Germany

Gevrey-Chambertin (Zhev-ray-Shahm-bair-*teng*) The largest commune in the Côte de Nuits

Gewürztraminer (Guh-*vürts*-tramee-ner) A superior quality Traminer

Gironde (Zhee-*rohnd*) The major river of Bordeaux

Givry (Zhee-*vree*) A commune in the Côte Chalonnaise

Goldtröpfchen (*Golt*-trupf-shen) The famous vineyard in Piesport (Moselle)

Goutte d'Or (Goot *Dor*) White *Premier Cru* in Meursault

Graach (Grahkh) A vineyard village of the Middle Moselle

Grand Cru (Grahng Krü) A great growth in Burgundy

Grands Echézeaux (Les) (Grahng Ay-sheh-*zo*) Red *Grand Cru* in Flagey-Echézeaux

Graves (Grahv) A red and white wine district of Bordeaux

Gravières (Les) (Grahv-*yair*) Red *Premier Cru* in Santenay

Grenouilles (Gruh-*nwee*) A *Grand Cru* in Chablis

Grèves (Les) (Grev) Red *Premier Cru* in Beaune

°**Grillet** (Gree-*yay*) A very small white wine estate in Condrieu (Rhône)

Grosslage (*Grohss*-la-guh) Area formed by neighboring German vineyards

°**Gruaud-Larose** (Grü-*oh*-La-rose) A Classified Second Growth in Médoc (St. Julien)

Grumello (Groo-*mel*-lo) A fine red wine from Valtellina (Lombardy)

°**Guiraud** (Ghee-*ro*) A Classified First Growth in Sauternes

Haro (*Ah*-ro) Chief town of Rio Alta

°**Haut-Bailly** (Oh-By-*yee*) A Classified Growth in Graves

~ (red)

*Haut-Brion (Oh-Bree-*yohng*) A Classified First Growth in Graves (red and white)

Hermitage (Air-mee-*tahzh*) Red wine area in the Côtes du Rhône

Himmelreich (*Him*-mel-rye'kh) The most famous vineyard in Graach (Moselle)

Hipping (*Hip*-ping) Most famous vineyard in Nierstein (Rheinhesse)

Hochheim (*Hohkh*-hime) The easternmost vineyard village of the Rheingau

Hospices de Beaune (*Oh*-spees duh *Bone)* The famous charity hospital in Beaune

Iberian (Eye-*bee*-ree-an) European Peninsula (Spain and Portugal)

Ile des Vergelesses (Eel day Vair-zher-*less*) Red *Premier Cru* in Pernand-Vergelesses

Inferno (Een-*fair*-no) A fine red wine from Valtellina (Lombardy)

*Issan (d') (Dee-*sahng*) A Classified Third Growth in Médoc (Margaux)

Jerez (Heh-*reth*) Sherry district in southern Spain

Johannisberg (Yo-ha-niss-bairg) A vineyard town in the Rheingau

Juliénas (Jül-*yay*-nahs) A commune in Beaujolais

Kabinett (Ka-bee-*nett*) Separate bottling of Qualitätswein mit Prädikat

Karthäuserhofberg (Kart-hoy-zer-*hohf*-bairg) An important estate in Eitelsbach (Saar)

Kellerabfüllung (*Kel*-ler-ahp-*fül*-loonk) Cellar bottling by the shipper

Kupfergrube (*Koop*-fer-*groo*-beh) An important vineyard in the Nahe

La (La) The, feminine article in French

Lacrima Christi (*La*-kree-ma *Kree*-stee) A still and sparkling white wine from Campania

*Lafite-Rothschild (La-*feet*-Rohts-*sheeld)* A Classified First Growth in Médoc (Pauillac)

*Lafon-Rochet (La-*fohng*-Ro-*shay)* A Classified Fourth Growth in Médoc (St. Estèphe)

Lake Garda (Lake *Gar*-da) Famous lake in Verona

La Mancha (La *Mahn*-chah) Largest volume wine district in Spain

Lambrusco (Lahm-*broo*-sko) A slightly sweet red wine from Emilia

Langlois-Château (Lahn-*glwah*-sha-*toh*) Leading producer of Sparkling Saumur

*Lascombes (Lahs-*kohm*) A Classified Second Growth in Médoc (Margaux)

La Tâche (La Tahsh) Red *Grand Cru* in Vosne-Romanée

Latium (*La*-tee-yum) A department in central Italy

*Latour (La-*toor*) A Classified First Growth in Médoc (Pauillac)

*La Tour-Blanche (La *Toor*-Blahngsh) A Classified First Growth (Sauternes)

Le (Luh) The, masculine article in French

Leiwen (*Lye*-ven) A vineyard village of the Middle Moselle

Lenchen (*Len*-shen) The most famous vineyard in Oestrich (Rheingau)

Léognan (Lay-oh-n'*yahng*) A principal parish in Graves

*Léoville-Barton (Lay-oh-*veel* Bar-*tohng*) A Classified Second Growth in Médoc (St. Julien)

Léoville-Las Cases (Lay-oh-*veel* Lahs-*kahz*) A Classified Second Growth in Médoc (St. Julien)

Léoville-Poyferré (Lay-oh-*veel* Pwa-fay-*ray*) A Classified Second Growth in Médoc (St. Julien)

Les (Lay) The, plural article in French

Liebfraumilch (*Leeb*-frow-milkh) The most popular Rhine wine

liqueur d'expédition (Lee-*kerr* dex-pay-dee-*s'yohng*) The shipping dosage in champagne that determines its dryness

Lirac (Lee-*rahk*) A *vin rosé* commune in the Côtes du Rhône

Logroño (Lo-*grohn*-yo) Chief town of Rioja Baja

Loire Valley (L'war Valley) Vineyard area along the Loire River

Lombardy (*Lom*-bar-dee) A department in northeast Italy

Mâcon (Ma-*kohng*) The principal town in the Côte Mâconnaise

Mâcon Blanc (Ma-*kohng* Blahng) White wine from the Côte Mâconnaise

Mâcon-Villages (Ma-*kohng* Vee-*lahzh*) Finer white wine from the Côte Mâconnaise

*Magdelaine** (Mahg-deh-*lain*) A Classified First Great Growth in St. Emilion

Málaga (*Ma*-la-ga) Sweet wine district in southern Spain

Malbec (Mahl-*bek*) A red wine grape of Bordeaux

*Malbec** (Mahl-*bek*) A Classified Growth in Premières Côtes de Bordeaux

*Marbuzet** (de) (Mar-bü-*zay*) Classified *Cru Exceptionnel* in Médoc (St. Estèphe)

marc (mark) Press loading in Champagne totaling four tons

Marche (*Mar*-kay) A department in east central Italy

Marcobrunn (Mar-ko-broon) The most famous vineyard in Erbach (Moselle)

Marconnets (Les) (Mar-ko-*nay*) A red *Premier Cru* in Beaune

Margaux (Mar-*go*) A principal parish in Haut-Médoc

*Margaux** (Mar-*go*) A Classified First Growth in Médoc (Margaux)

Marsala (Mar-*sa*-la) A sweet fortified wine from Sicily

"Marseillaise" ("La") (Mar-say-*yaze*) The French national anthem

Martillac (Mar-tee-*yahk*) A principal parish in Graves

Marzo (*Mar*-tho) Spanish for dry land (La Mancha)

Maximin Grünhaus (Max-zee-*min* Grün-howss) An important estate in Mertesdorf (Saar)

Mazis-Chambertin (Ma-*zee* Shahm-bair-*teng*) Red *Grand Cru* in Gevrey-Chambertin

Médoc (May-*dohk*) The major red wine district of Bordeaux

Mercurey (Mair-kü-*rey*) A commune in the Côte Chalonnaise

Merlot (Mair-*lo*) A red wine grape of Bordeaux

Meursault (Merr-*so*) A white wine commune in the Côte de Beaune

*Mission-Haut-Brion** (La) (Mees-*yohng* Oh-Bree-*yohng*) A Classified Growth in Graves (red)

Mistela (Mee-*steh*-la) Unfermented must used in Rioja

Mit Prädikat (Mitt Pray-dee-*kaht*) Superior grade of Qualitätswein

Montagny (Mohng-tahn-*yee*) A commune in the Côte Chalonnaise

Montefiascone (Mohn-te-f'*yahs*-ko-nay) Vineyard town on Lake Bolsena in Latium

Montilla (Mohn-*teel*-ya) Sherry-type district in southern Spain

Montrachet (Mohng-tra-*shay*) White *Grand Cru* in Puligny-Montrachet

Monthélie (Mohng-tay-*lee*) Small red wine commune in the Côte de Beaune

***Montrose** (Mohng-*rose*) A Classified Second Growth in Médoc (St. Estèphe)

Monts des Milieu (Mohng duh Meel-*yuh*) A *Premier Cru* in Chablis

Morey-St. Denis (Mo-ray Sahng Duh-*nee*) Small red wine commune in the Côte de Nuits

Morgon (More-*gohng*) A commune in Beaujolais

Moselblümchen (*Mo*-sel-blüm-chen) A blended wine—"little flower of the Moselle"

Moulin-à-Vent (Moo-leng-ah-*Vahng*) The best-known commune in Beaujolais

***Mouton-Rothschild** (Moo-tohng-Roht-*sheel*) A Classified First Growth in Médoc (Pauillac)

Muscadet (Müss-ka-*day*) Vineyard region of the Loire Valley

Musigny (Les) (Mü-zeen-*yee*) Red *Grand Cru* in Chambolle-Musigny

Nahe (*Na*-heh) A vineyard area of the Rhine

Nebbiolo (Nebb-*yo*-lo) A red wine grape of Italy

Négociant (Nay-gohs-*yahng*) A Bordeaux wine shipper

Nierstein (*Neer*-shtine) A vineyard village of the Rheinhesse

Nuits-St. Georges (N'wee Seng-*Zhorzh*) A red wine commune in the Côte de Nuits

Oestrich (Err-*strikh*) A vineyard village of the Rheingau

***Olivier** (Oh-leev-*yay*) A Classified Growth in Graves (white and red)

Ollauri (Ohl-*yow*-ree) Small town in Rioja Alta

Oppenheim (*Ohp*-pen-hime) A vineyard village of the Rein-hesse

Orvieto Abboccato (Orv-*yay*-toh Ahb-bo-*ka*-toh) Slightly fruity white wine from Umbria

Orvieto Secco (Orv-*yay*-toh Sek-ko) Dry white wine from Umbria

Palatinate (Rheinpfalz) (Pa-*la*-tee-nate) A vineyard area of the Rhine

Palazzo Antinori (Pa-*laht*-so Ahn-tee-*no*-ree) The Renaissance Antinori building (Florence)

Palette (Pa-*let*) A red wine appellation in Côtes de Provence

***Palmer** (Pahl-*mair*) A Classified Third Growth in Médoc (Margaux)

paniers (pahn-*yay*) Baskets used by grape pickers in Champagne

***Pape-Clément** (Pahp Clay-*mahng*) A Classified Growth in Graves (red)

Passe-tous-grains (Pahss-too-Greng) A red wine made from both Pinot Noir and Gamay

Paternina (Pa-tay-*nee*-na) Leading shipper of quality Rioja

Paterno (Pa-*tair*-no) Antinori estate in Classico Chianti

Pauillac (Poh-*yahk*) A principal parish in the Haut-Médoc

***Pavie** (Pa-*vee*) A Classified First Great Growth in St. Emilion

Pelligo (Pel-*yee*-go) Wine container from skin of a pig

Pernand-Vergelesses (Pair-nahng-Vair-zhuh-*less*) A red wine commune in the Côte de Beaune

Pessac (Pess-*sahk*) A principal parish in Graves

Petit Chablis (Puh-tee Sha-*blee*) A lesser appellation in Chablis

***Petit-Village** (Puh-tee Vee-*lahzh*) A First Growth in Pomerol

***Pétrus** (Pay-trüss) A First Great Growth in Pomerol

***Phélan-Ségur** (Fay-*lahng*-Say-gür) A *Cru Bourgeois Exceptionnel* in Médoc (St. Estèphe)

phylloxera (Fy-*lox*-eh-ra) Native American plant lice

Piazza Antinori (P'*yaht*-sa Ahn-tee-*no*-ree) The Antinori "square" in Florence

***Pichon-Lalande** (Pee-*shohng*-La-*lahnd*) A classified Second Growth in Médoc (Pauillac)

***Pichon-Longueville** (Pee-*shohng*-Long-veel) A Classified Second Growth in Médoc (Pauillac)

Pichon-Longueville-Lalande (Pee-*shohng*-Long-veel-Lah-*lahnd*) A Classified Second Growth in Médoc (Pauillac)

Piedmont (*Peed*-mont) A department in northeast Italy

Piesport (*Peess*-port) Vineyard village of the Middle Moselle

Pinot Chardonnay (Pee-*no* Shardoh-*nay*) The noble white grape of Burgundy

Pinot Noir (Pee-*no* N'war) The noble red grape of Burgundy

***Piron** (Pee-*rohng*) A Classified Principal Growth in Graves

Pomerol (Po-may-*rol*) A red wine district of Bordeaux

Pommard (Po-*mar*) The best-known commune in the Côte de Beaune

Portoferraio (Por-toh-feh-*ra*-yo) Antinori estate on Elba

Pouilly-Fuissé (Poo-*yee*-Fwee-say) Famous white wine from the Côte Mâconnaise

Pouilly-Fumé (Poo-yee-Fü-*may*) The important wine from the Loire Valley

Pouilly-Loché (Poo-*yee*-Loh-*shay*) White wine commune in the Côte Mâconnaise

Pouilly-sur-Loire (Poo-*yee* sür L'war) White wine vineyard town in the Loire Valley

Pouilly-Vinzelles (Poo-*yee* Veng-zel) White wine commune in the Côte Mâconnaise

Prats (Prahts) Leading producer and shipper (Bordeaux)

Prémeaux (Pray-*mo*) Red wine commune in the Côte de Nuits

première taille (pruh-m'yair tie) The second pressing in Champagne

Preuses (Les) (Pruhz) A *Grand Cru* in Chablis

Provence (Pro-*vahngss*) The vineyard region of the French Riviera

Puligny-Montrachet (Pü-leen-*yee*-Mohng-tra-*shay*) White wine commune in the Côte de Beaune

pupitres (pu-*peetr*) Slanting cellar racks used in Champagne

Qualitätswein (Kva-lee-*taits*-vine) Superior German table wine

Quarts-de-Chaume (Kar-duh-Showm) Small white wine appellation in Anjou-Saumur

Quincy (Keng-*see*) Small vineyard town in the central Loire Valley

***Rausan-Ségla** (Roh-sahng Say-*gla*) A Classified Second Growth in Médoc (Margaux)

***Rauzan-Gassies** (Roh-sahng Gas-*see*) A Classified Second Growth in Médoc (Margaux)

***Rayne-Vigneau (de)** (duh Rain-veen-*yo*) A Classified First Growth in Sauternes

rebêche (ruh-*besh*) The fourth pressing in Champagne

Reims (Rengss) The capital of

the champagne region

remuage (ruh-m'wahzh) Jiggling champagne in secondary fermentation

Reserva (Ray-*sair*-va) Designates fine old Rioja wines

Reuilly (Roy-*yee*) Small vineyard town in the central Loire Valley

Rheims (Rengss) The capital of the Champagne region

Rheingau (*Rine*-gow) A vineyard area of the Rhine

Rheinhesse (*Rine*-hess-seh) A vineyard area of the Rhine

Rheinpfalz (**Palatinate**) (*Rine*-pfahlts) A vineyard area of the Rhine

Richebourg (**Le**) (Reesh-*boor*) Red *Grand Cru* in Vosne-Romanée

Riesling (Rees-ling) The noble grape in Alsace and Germany

*****Rieussec** (R'yuh-*sek*) A Classified First Growth in Sauternes

Rioja Alavesa (Ree-*yo*-ha Ah-la-*vay*-sa) Good quality district in Rioja

Rioja Alta (Ree-*yo*-ha *Ahl*-ta) Finest wine district in Rioja

Rioja Baja (Ree-*yo*-ha *Ba*-ha) Lesser wine district in Rioja

Rio Ebro (Ree-yo *Eh*-bro) River in Rioja Valley

Rioja (*Ree*-yo-ha) Finest quality wine region in Spain

Rio Oja (*Ree*-yo *Oh*-ha) Small river in western Rioja

Romanée (**La**) (Ro-ma-*nay*) Red *Grand Cru* in Vosne-Romanée

Romanée-Conti (**La**) (Ro-ma-*nay*-Kohn-*tee*) Red *Grand Cru* in Vosne-Romanée

Romanée-St.-Vivant (Ro-may-*nay* Seng-Vee-*vahng*) Red *Grand Cru* in Vosne-Romanée

Rosé d'Anjou (Ro-zay dahn-*zhoo*) A *vin rosé* from Anjou (Loire)

Rotenfels (*Ro*-ten-fels) An important vineyard in the Nahe

Rudesheim (*Roo*-dess-hime) Westernmost vineyard village of the Rheingau

Rudesheimer Berg (*Roo*-dess-hime-er Bairg) Finest vineyards in Rudesheim (Rheingau)

Rugiens (**Les**) (Ru-*zheng*) Red *Premier Cru* in Pommard

Rully (Rü-*yee*) A commune in the Côte Chalonnaise

Ruwer (*Ru*-ver) A vineyard area of the Upper Moselle

Saar (Zar) A vineyard area of the Upper Moselle

Sancerre (Sahng-*sair*) A vineyard town in the central Loire Valley

Santa Cristina (Sahn-ta Kree-*stee*-na) Antinori estate in Classico Chianti

Santenay (Sahn-tuh-*nay*) Southernmost commune in the Côte de Beaune

Santenots (**Les**) (Sahn-tuh-*no*) Red *Premier Cru* in Volnay

Sassella (Sahs-*sel*-la) A fine red wine from Valtellina (Lombardy)

Saumur (So-*mür*) An important white wine of the Loire Valley

Sauternes (So-*tairn*) White wine region of Bordeaux

Sauvignon Blanc (So-vee-yohng *Blahng*) Major white wine grape of the Graves

Savennières (Sa-ven-*yair*) A small appellation in Anjou-Saumur

Savigny-les-Beaune (Sa-veen-*yee*-lay-*Bone*) Red wine commune in the Côte de Beaune

Scharzhof (*Sharts*-hohf) A famous estate in Wiltingen (Saar)

Schloss Johannisberg (Shlohss Yo-*ha*-nis-bairg) Most famous vineyard of Johannisberg (Rheingau)

Schloss Vollrads (Shlohss *Fohl-*

rahts) Most famous vineyard of Winkel (Rheingau)

Sec (Sek) The next-to-sweetest champagne

Sémillon (Say-mee-*yohng*) Major grape of the Sauternes

Sicily (*Sis*-sil-ly) Island department at southern tip of Italy

Sierra Cantabria (S'yair-ra Kahn-*ta*-bree-ya) Mountains protecting Rioja Valley

Soave (So-*ah*-vay) A Veronese white wine

Solutré (So-lü-*tray*) White wine village in the Côte Mâconnais

Sonnenuhr (*Zoh*-nen-oor) Most famous vineyard in Wehlen (Moselle)

Spätlese (*Shpayt*-lay-seh) Late-picked fully ripened grapes

Steinberg (*Shtine*-bairg) Most famous vineyard in Hattenheim (Rheingau)

Steinwein (*Shtine*-vine) The generic name for Franconian wines

St.-Amour (Seng Ta-*moor*) The northernmost commune in Beaujolais

St. Emilion (Seng-tay-meel-*yohng*) Red wine district of Bordeaux

St. Estèphe (Seng-tes-*teff*) A principal parish in the Haut-Médoc

St. Julien (Seng zhül-*yahng*) A principal parish in the Haut-Médoc

*Ste. Roseline (Sahnt Rose-*leen*) The foremost château-bottled *vin rosé* (Provence)

Strasbourg (Strahss-*boor*) The capital of Alsace

Sylvaner (Sil-*va*-ner) White wine grape used in Alsace and Germany

Syrah (See-*ra*) Red wine grape of the Côtes du Rhône

Tafelwein (*Tah*-fel-vine) Ordinary German table wine

*Talbot (Tahl-*bo*) A Classified Fourth Growth in Médoc (St. Julien)

Talence (Ta-*lahnce*) A principal parish in Graves

Tarragona (Tar-ra-*go*-na) Largest volume wine district in northeast Spain

*Tastes (de) (Tahst) A Classified Growth in Sainte-Croix-du-Mont

Tavel (Ta-*vel*) *Vin rosé* commune in the Côtes du Rhône

Teurons (Les) (Toor-*ohng*) Red *Premier Cru* in Beaune

Tiergarten (*Teer*-gar-ten) All-important vineyard in Trier (Ruwer)

Traminer (Tra-*meen*-ehr) White wine grape used mainly in Alsace

Trier (*Tree*-yer) An important city on the Moselle

Trockenbeeren (*Tro*-ken-beh-ren) Semidried or shriveled grapes

Tuscany (*Tuss*-ca-nee) A department in central Italy

Umbria (*Oom*-bree-ya) A west central department of Italy

Valdepeñas (Vahl-day-*pain*-yahs) Chief wine town in La Mancha

Valmur (Vahl-*mür*) A *Grand Cru* in Chablis

Valpolicella (Vahl-po-lee-*chel*-la) Veronese red wine

Valtellina (Vahl-tel-*lee*-na) A red wine region in northern Lombardy

Valtenesi (Vahl-teh-*nay*-zee) A vineyard area on Lake Garda (Lombardy)

Vaudésir (Vo-day-*zeer*) A *Grand Cru* in Chablis

Verdicchio (Vair-*deek*-yo) A pale white wine from Marche

Vergisson (Vair-zhee-*sohng*) A white wine village in the Côte Mâconnaise

Verona (Veh-*ro*-na) A department

in northern Italy

*Vieux-Château-Certan (V'yuh-Sha-*toh*-Sair-*tahng*) A First Great Growth in Pomerol

Villa Antinori (Vee-la Ahn-tee-*no*-ree) Estate-bottled Classico Chianti

Villa Riserva (Vee-la Ree-*zair*-va) Special Reserve of Villa Antinori

Villefranche (Veel-*frahnsh*) Main city of Beaujolais

Vin Rosé (Veng Ro-*zay*) A light rose-colored wine

Vino dell'Elba (*Vee*-no del Elba) A light white wine from Elba

Vin Santo (Veen *Sahn*-toh) A white dessert wine from Tuscany

Voignier (Vwahn-*yay*) White wine grape of the Côtes du Rhône

Volnay (Vohl-*nay*) Red wine commune in Côte de Beaune

Volnay-Santenots (Vohl-nay Sahn-tuh-*no*) Red *Premier Cru* in Volnay

Vosges Mountains (Vohzh Mountains) Mountains on western border of Alsace

Vosne-Romanée (Vone Ro-ma-*nay*) Red wine commune in the Côte de Nuits

Vougeot (Voo-*zhoh*) Red wine commune in the Côte de Nuits

Vouvray (Voov-*ray*) Important white wine in the Coteaux de Touraine

Wehlen (*Vay*-len) A vineyard village in the Middle Moselle

Willm (Vill'm) Leading producer and shipper (Alsace)

Wiltingen (*Vil*-tin-gen) The important vineyard village of the Saar

Winkel (*Vin*-kel) A vineyard village of the Rheingau

Würzburg (*Vürts*-boorg) The main city of Franconia

*Yquem (d') (Dee-*kem*) The Classified Superior First Growth (Sauternes)

Zell (Tsell) A vineyard village of the Middle Moselle

Zeller Schwarze Katz (*Tsell*-er *Shvar*-tseh Kahtz) The "black cat" wine from Zell (Moselle)

Zeltingen (*Tsel*-ting-en) A large vineyard town on the Moselle

Appendix

OFFICIAL CLASSIFICATION OF 1855

First Growths

Château Lafite-Rothschild
Château Margaux
Château Latour

Château Haut-Brion
Château Mouton-Rothschild

Second Growths

Château Cos d'Estournel
Château Rausan-Ségla
Château Rauzan-Gassies
Château Léoville-Las Cases
Château Léoville-Poyferré
Château Léoville-Barton
Château Durfort-Vivens
Château Gruaud-Larose

Château Lascombes
Château Brane-Cantenac
Château Pichon-Longueville
Château Pichon-Longueville-
  Lalande
Château Ducru-Beaucaillou
Château Montrose

Third Growths

Château Kirwan
Château d'Issan
Château Lagrange
Château Langoa-Barton
Château Giscours
Château Malescot-St.-Exupéry
Château Boyd-Cantenac
Château Cantenac-Brown

Château Palmer
Château La Lagune
Château Desmirail
Château Calon-Ségur
Château Ferrière
Château Marquis-d'Alesme-
  Becker

Fourth Growths

Château St.-Pierre
Château Talbot
Château Branaire-Ducru
Château Duhart-Milon
Château Pouget

Château La Tour-Carnet
Château Lafon-Rochet
Château Beychevelle
Château Prieuré-Lichine
Château Marquis-de-Terme

Fifth Growths

Château Pontet-Canet
Château Batailley
Château Haut-Batailley
Château Grand-Puy-Lacoste
Château Grand-Puy-Ducasse
Château Lynch-Bages
Château Lynch-Moussas
Château Dauzac
Château Mouton-Baron-
   Philippe

Château du Tertre
Château Haut-Bages-Libéral
Château Pédesclaux
Château Belgrave
Château Camensac
Château Cos-Labory
Château Clerc-Milon-Mondon
Château Croizet-Bages
Château Cantemerle

SAUTERNES AND BARSAC
Superior First Growth
Château d'Yquem

First Growths

Château La Tour-Blanche
Château Lafaurie-Peyraguey
Clos Haut-Peyraguey
Château de Rayne-Vigneau
Château de Suduiraut
Château Coutet

Château Climens
Château Guiraud
Château Rieussec
Château Rabaud-Promis
Château Sigalas-Rabaud

Second Growths

Château Myrat
Château Doisy-Daëne
Château Doisy
Château Doisy-Védrines
Château d'Arche
Château Filhot
Château Broustet

Château Nairac
Château Caillou
Château Suau
Château de Malle
Château Romer
Château Lamothe

OFFICIAL CLASSIFICATION OF 1953—GRAVES

Classified Red Wines

Château Bouscaut
Château Carbonnieux
Domaine de Chevalier
Château de Fieuzal
Château Haut-Bailly
Château Haut-Brion
Château La Mission-Haut-
  Brion

Château La Tour-Haut-Brion
Château Kressman La Tour
Château Malartic-Lagravière
Château Olivier
Château Pape-Clément
Château Smith-Haut-Lafitte

Classified White Wines

Château Bouscaut
Château Carbonnieux
Domaine de Chevalier
Château Couhins
Château Haut-Brion

Château Kressman La Tour
Château Laville-Haut-Brion
Château Malartic-Lagravière
Château Olivier

UNOFFICIAL CLASSIFICATION OF POMEROL

Great First Growths

Château Pétrus

Vieux-Château Certan

First Growths

Château Certan-de-May
Château Gazin
Château La Conseillante
Château La Croix
Château Lafleur
Château Lafleur-Pétrus
Château Lagrange
Clos l'Eglise
Château Clos René

Château Latour-Pomerol
Château l'Eglise-Clinet
Château l'Evangile
Château Nénin
Château Petit-Village
Château Rouget
Château Trotanoy
Château Le Gay
Château La Croix-de-Gay

OFFICIAL CLASSIFICATION OF 1955—ST. EMILION

First Great Classified Growths (a)

Château Ausone

Château Cheval Blanc

First Great Classified Growths (b)

Château Beauséjour-Duffau-
   Lagarosse
Château Beauséjour-Fagouet
Château Belair
Château Canon
Clos Fourtet

Château Figeac
Château La Gaffelière
Château Magdelaine
Château Pavie
Château Trottevieille

Great Classified Growths

Château l'Angélus
Château l'Arrosée
Château Balestard-la-Tonnelle
Château Cadet-Piola
Château Canon-la-Gaffelière
Château Cap de Mourlin
Château Chappelle-Madelaine
Château Corbin
Château Croque-Michotte
Château Curé-Bon-la-Made-
   leine
Château Fonplégade
Château Fonroque
Château Grand-Corbin

Château Guadet-Saint-Julien
Clos des Jacobins
Château La Clotte
Château La Dominique
Château Larcis-Ducasse
Château La Tour-du-Pin-
   Figeac
Château La Tour-Figeac
Château Petit Figeac
Château Ripeau
Château Soutard
Château Troplong-Mondot
Château Villemaurine

THE PRINCIPAL VINEYARDS OF THE
COTE DE NUITS

NUITS-SAINT-GEORGES
Les St.-Georges
Les Cailles
Les Porrets

VOSNE-ROMANEE
Le Richebourg
La Romanée
La Romanée-Conti
La Tâche
Romanée-St.-Vivant

FLAGEY-ECHEZEAUX
Les Echézeaux
Les Grands Echézeaux

VOUGEOT
Clos de Vougeot

CHAMBOLLE-MUSIGNY
Les Musigny
Les Bonnes Mares
Les Charmes
Les Amoureuses

MOREY-ST. DENIS
Clos de Tart
St. Denis
Clos de la Roche

GEVREY-CHAMBERTIN
Chambertin
Clos de Bèze
Charmes-Chambertin
Chapelle-Chambertin
Griotte-Chambertin
Latricières-Chambertin
Mazis-Chambertin

FIXIN
Les Hervelets
La Perrière

THE PRINCIPAL VINEYARDS OF THE COTE DE BEAUNE

SANTENAY
Les Gravières
La Comme

CHASSAGNE-MONTRA-CHET
Clos St.-Jean
Morgeot

PULIGNY-MONTRACHET
Le Montrachet
Chevalier-Montrachet
Bâtard-Montrachet
Les Bienvenues
Les Criots

MEURSAULT
La Goutte-d'Or
Les Charmes

VOLNAY
Caillerets
Champans

POMMARD
Les Epenots
Les Rugiens

BEAUNE
Les Grèves
Les Fèves
Les Marconnets
Les Teurons
Le Clos des Mouches

SAVIGNY-LES-BEAUNE
La Dominode

PERNAND-VERGELESSES
Ile des Vergelesses
Les Vergelesses

ALOXE-CORTON
Le Corton
Les Renardes
Le Clos du Roi
Les Bressandes
Les Pougets
Corton-Charlemagne

HOSPICES DE BEAUNE
RED WINES

CUVEE	COMMUNE
Arthur Girard	Savigny-les-Beaune
Billardet	Pommard
Blondeau	Volnay
Boillot	Auxey-Duresses
Brunet	Beaune
Charlotte Dumay	Aloxe-Corton
Clos des Avaux	Beaune
Dames de la Charité	Pommard
Dames Hospitalières	Beaune
Docteur Peste	Aloxe-Corton
Du Bay-Peste-Cyrot	Savigny-les-Beaune
Estiènne	Beaune
Forneret	Savigny-les-Beaune
Fouquerand	Savigny-les-Beaune
Gauvain	Volnay
Guigone de Salins	Beaune
Henri Gelicot	Monthélie
Huges et Louis Bétault	Beaune
Jacques Lebelin	Monthélie
Jehan de Massol	Volnay
Maurice Drouhin	Beaune
Nicolas Rolin	Beaune
Pierre Virely	Beaune
Rousseau Deslandes	Beaune

WHITE WINES

CUVEE	COMMUNE
Albert Grivault	Meursault
de Bahèzre de Lanlay	Meursault
Baudot	Meursault
Francois de Salins	Aloxe-Corton
Goureau	Meursault
Jehan Humblot	Meursault
Loppin	Meursault
Philippe Le Bon	Meursault

About the Author

Howard L. Blum was born in Brooklyn, New York, into a family with a long history in the wine business. His father, grandfather and great-grandfather were all associated with Julius Wile Sons & Co., Inc., the outstanding importer of fine wines and spirits, which was founded in 1877.

Mr. Blum attended Horace Mann School for Boys and was graduated cum laude from Haverford College in 1941, where he played on the varsity soccer, squash and tennis teams. Commissioned an Ensign in the United States Naval Reserve in September 1941, he served on three different aircraft carriers in 14 major naval engagements in the Pacific.

Upon his release to inactive service as a Lieutenant Commander, he joined the family firm. His entire business career has been in selling imported wines, first in the New York market and then in all other major markets throughout the United States. Today, as Senior Vice President and General Sales Manager of Julius Wile Sons & Co., Inc., he directs the sales of all the prestigious brands of imported wines and liqueurs, for which the company is the sole U.S. importer.

Mr. Blum lives with his wife Janine in Chappaqua, New York, in a hundred-year-old house they have been restoring and remodeling. An active sportsman, his favorite sports are golf, horseback riding and upland game shooting.